T0113872

THE LIFE

A BIOGRAPHICAL STUDY OF
THE LIFE OF JESUS CHRIST

DANA L. GOODNOUGH

WESTBOW
PRESS®
A DIVISION OF THOMAS NELSON
& ZONDERVAN

WestBow Press books may be ordered through
booksellers or by contacting:

WestBow Press
A Division of Thomas Nelson & Zondervan
1663 Liberty Drive
Bloomington, IN 47403
www.westbowpress.com
844-714-3454

Scripture quotations are taken from The Holy Bible, New International
Version®, NIV® Copyright © 1973, 1978, 1984, 2011 by Biblica,
Inc.® Used by permission. All rights reserved worldwide.

ISBN: 978-1-6642-8660-3 (sc)
ISBN: 978-1-6642-8659-7 (e)

Print information available on the last page.

WestBow Press rev. date: 12/30/2022

CONTENTS

INTRODUCTION

There is no life that compares to that of Jesus Christ. He made a greater impact on this world than anyone else in history. Jesus taught greater truths than the greatest of philosophers and scholars. He showed a level of humility and compassion that far exceeds any humanitarian. He healed the sick, raised the dead, calmed the seas, fed the multitudes, and gave His life for His enemies. Jesus lived a perfect life, provided a perfect sacrifice for our sins, and rose triumphantly from the dead. Jesus Christ is like no other. His life is well worthy of our study, reflection, and imitation.

The life of Jesus Christ is recorded in the four Gospels of the New Testament. These four accounts—Matthew, Mark, Luke, and John—each provide unique contributions toward the study of the life of Jesus. Taken together, the four Gospels paint a brilliant portrait.

Although the four Gospels provide our only authoritative information about the life of Jesus Christ, none of the four presents a complete or detailed biography. We don't know precisely when Jesus was born, although we know He was born prior to the death of Herod the Great around 4 B.C. We don't know the exact year of

His death, although most scholars point to either A.D. 30 or 33. We don't know much about Jesus' life between His birth and His arrival on the public scene. The Gospel writers weren't interested in these details. They were interested in presenting the essential purpose of Jesus' life. Jesus came to serve and to save (Mark 10:45).

Any effort at reconstructing the life of Jesus Christ must account for the similarities and distinct contributions of the four Gospels. The three Synoptic Gospels—Matthew, Mark, and Luke—present similar material and, apart from the thematic section in Matthew (5:1—13:58), present a similar chronological flow of events. Luke's "Travel Narrative" (9:52—18:14) provides additional material not recorded by Matthew or Mark, including three references to journeys Jesus made to Jerusalem (or possibly three references to Jesus' final journey to Jerusalem).

The Gospel of John stands out among the four Gospels in the uniqueness of its content and presentation. John alone gives reference to several feasts that Jesus attended, helping us to understand that Jesus' ministry took place over a period of three or more years. John also refers to three journeys Jesus took to Jerusalem, possibly corresponding to the three journeys in Luke's Gospel. These unique accounts further enhance the chronological framework of the life of Jesus.

One key to weaving together the three Synoptic Gospels with the unique material of John's Gospel is found in Jesus' miracle of feeding the five thousand. Apart from Jesus' resurrection, this is the only miracle recorded in all four Gospels. It, therefore, provides a chronological link between the four accounts of Jesus' ministry. In addition, if we take the three references to later Jerusalem journeys in Luke's Gospel (9:51; 13:22; 17:11) and link them with the three references to Jerusalem journeys in John's Gospel (7:2; 11:17; 12:1), we can arrive at a reasonably accurate account of Jesus' public ministry from beginning to end.

Various approaches to outlining the life of Jesus have been devised over the years, but the most memorable seem to be those that tie Jesus' activities into a geographical structure. Jesus began His work in Judea, moved north to Galilee for an extended period of ministry, and then concluded his public ministry in Perea and Judea. Jesus' lengthy ministry in Galilee is often divided into three parts—early, middle, and later phases. Jesus' journeys to Jerusalem to celebrate special feasts provide helpful markers in distinguishing between these three phases of His Galilean ministry. The great Galilean ministry also includes at least seven distinct itinerant tours throughout that region, again providing a geographical structure to Jesus' work. All four Gospels provide extensive information about Jesus' final week, the Passion week, leading up to His crucifixion and resurrection. Jesus' redemptive work clearly forms the climax to His life and ministry.

A useful practice in studying the life of Jesus is to group together identifiable units of activity from the four Gospels. A distinct unit or event in the life of Jesus is often referred to as a "pericope." There is no standardized identification of the various pericopes in Jesus' life, but we can distinguish well over two hundred such units of activity. These are designated by a gothic "p," (𝔭) in this volume.

Based on the details found in the four Gospels, we

can outline the life and ministry of Jesus as follows: (1) The Birth and Childhood of Jesus, (2) The Early Judean and Samarian Ministry, (3) The Early Galilean Ministry, (4) The Middle Galilean Ministry, (5) The Later Galilean Ministry, (6) The Later Judean and Perean Ministry, (7) The Death and Resurrection of Jesus.

Some events in the life of Jesus capture our imagination more readily than others. After all, who doesn't have a favorite miracle or parable in the Gospels? However, every event in Jesus' life is important. Certainly every individual who was healed by Jesus' touch would see his or her encounter as highly significant! Likewise, every word spoken by Jesus carries spiritual authority in our lives. For this reason, this volume attempts to sketch every event in Jesus' life as recorded in the four Gospels.

Obviously, such a brief treatment will fail to do justice to the greatness of our Lord. His life deserves a lifetime of reflection. His words deserve a lifelong commitment to study and obedience. But the journey to understand Jesus better can begin with a simple overview of His life, the greatest life ever lived.

1

THE BIRTH AND CHILDHOOD OF JESUS

GOD ENTERED THE WORLD—THIS IS THE CENTRAL truth of the life of Jesus Christ. God entered the world in the person of Jesus. Jesus came from heaven and made His entrance into this world in a lowly stable. God became a man in order to bring men and women to God. Our study of the life of Jesus Christ begins naturally with His birth and childhood, but it really begins in eternity past, because Jesus is more than just a man. He is God in the flesh, deity incarnated.

The Incarnation of Jesus Christ

The incarnation of Jesus Christ was that historical event in which God took on a human nature. God and man were forever joined in one person, Jesus Christ.

#1—THE EYEWITNESS SOURCE OF THE GOSPEL RECORD (LUKE 1:1-4).

Of the four Gospel writers, Luke especially wanted to establish the historical nature of Jesus' life. Therefore, Luke began his account by assuring his readers that he himself had "carefully investigated" everything he wrote about. He gathered his information about Jesus' life from a variety of eyewitness reports and presented these accounts in an orderly fashion. Luke was a meticulous historian, so we can be sure that what he wrote is accurate. In fact, all four Gospels provide inspired, accurate accounts of the life of Jesus Christ.

#2—THE PRE-EXISTENCE AND INCARNATION OF JESUS CHRIST (JOHN 1:1-14).

Rather than start with a description of his historical research like Luke, John begins his Gospel by describing the pre-existence and incarnation of Jesus Christ. John pulls back the curtain of eternity and reveals to us the fact that Jesus has always existed. He is God. John describes the pre-incarnate Jesus as "the Word," the absolute and perfect expression of deity. John tells us that "the Word," Jesus, was "with God." Jesus was with God the Father long before He entered into His human existence. This means that Jesus had an eternal, face to face relationship with God the Father. Furthermore, John declares that "the Word," Jesus, was and is Himself "God." Here we have an indication of the triune nature of God as Father, Son, and Holy Spirit. Jesus was with God, and He is God. He was not created but created all things. He possesses life in and of Himself, and He has given us life. However, even though Jesus created us, we have rejected Him. We've turned away from God through sin. Therefore, God enacted His eternal plan of rescuing us from our sin. As the second member of the mysterious, triune Godhead, Jesus became a human being. He who is truly God became truly human. This act of Jesus Christ in becoming human is called the incarnation. Jesus took on a human nature, minus human sin, and lived among us. He did so in order to die for our sins and restore us to eternal life. Jesus opened the way for us to return to a relationship with God. But we, as John tells us in his magnificent prologue to the fourth Gospel, must receive Jesus, believing that He is truly God, that He truly died for our sins, and that we can truly and eternally be forgiven and restored to a relationship with Him. This is, indeed, good news—very good news, the gospel of Jesus Christ!

#3—THE GENEALOGIES OF JESUS (MATTHEW 1:1-17; LUKE 3:23-38).

It's essential for us to begin our journey into the life of Jesus Christ by understanding His eternal preexistence as God. But we must also come to appreciate Jesus' humanity. For this reason, both Matthew and Luke record the human genealogy of Jesus. Matthew traces Jesus' human ancestry beginning with Abraham, the Father of Faith, and working his way forward from Abraham through King David and eventually to Mary and Joseph. It was through Mary that Jesus was born. Jesus, therefore, is truly human with a human genealogy. Luke likewise presents the genealogy of Jesus but begins with Joseph and works backward through time to King David, Abraham, and eventually the first human being, Adam. Once again, we're impressed with the fact that Jesus has a human lineage. He is God and He became a man. Careful students of the Bible will observe that the two genealogies in Matthew and Luke are quite different. This is no cause for concern. We all have two distinct genealogies, one through our father and one through our mother. Matthew may indeed be presenting the genealogy of Joseph, Jesus' adoptive and legal human father. Luke, on the other hand, may be presenting Mary's genealogy. The important point to bear in mind is the fact that Jesus, who is eternally God, took on a truly human nature at a particular point in human history. Jesus is now God and man in one.

4—THE PREDICTION OF THE BIRTH OF JOHN THE BAPTIST (LUKE 1:5-25).

Before Jesus entered into His human existence, God paved the way by raising up a mighty prophet, a forerunner who would announce the arrival of this divine-human Messiah. This forerunner was John the Baptist. Luke describes the way in which John's birth came about. John's father was an aged priest named Zechariah. Zechariah and his wife Elizabeth were devout in their faith but had been unable over the years to have a child. In their advanced years of life the angel Gabriel appeared to Zechariah while this priest was performing his priestly functions at the Temple in Jerusalem. Gabriel informed Zechariah that he and Elizabeth would have a son who would be a powerful prophet like Elijah of old. This son would introduce God's Messiah to the world. Of course, Zechariah was stunned by this angelic visitation and expressed his doubts to Gabriel. As a sign of the veracity of his message, Gabriel temporarily took away Zechariah's ability to speak. Having completed his priestly duties, Zechariah took Elizabeth back to their own village. Soon it became apparent that Elizabeth was going to have a child. Gabriel's prediction had come true.

5—THE ANNUNCIATION TO MARY (LUKE 1:26-38).

Shortly after appearing to Zechariah, Gabriel had another amazing message to deliver. This time God sent Gabriel to a humble virgin living in Nazareth, a tiny town in Galilee. This virgin's name was Mary. Gabriel assured Mary of God's presence in her life and assured her that she need not be afraid. In fact, she should rejoice because she had found special favor in God's sight. Gabriel informed Mary that she would soon be expecting a child, a son, whom she was to name Jesus, meaning Savior. This son, Jesus, would be no ordinary child. He would come to be known as "the Son of the Most High," that is, the Son of God. Jesus would become the fulfillment of the Old Testament prophecies, ruling on David's throne forever.

Mary, of course, was deeply puzzled by this angelic prediction. She asked Gabriel how she could possibly have a child since she was a virgin. Gabriel assured Mary that God was going to do a supernatural work in her life. The Holy Spirit of God would engender life in her womb. This son of Mary would also be the Son of God. Unlike the accounts of mythological gods who often took advantage of humble maidens, the account of Mary's miraculous conception is filled with purity and holiness. God created human life in Mary's womb, miraculously and eternally joining Jesus' divine and human natures. Mary humbly accepted the angel's announcement and said, "I am the Lord's servant." She submitted herself to the will of God, and God blessed Mary by allowing her to become the mother of Jesus.

#6—MARY'S VISIT TO ELIZABETH (LUKE 1:39-45).

Gabriel had informed Mary that one of her older relatives, Elizabeth, was going to have a baby as well. Mary went to visit Elizabeth and her husband Zechariah, who lived in Judea. When Mary arrived at Elizabeth's house, the baby in Elizabeth's womb leaped for joy! This baby was, of course, John the Baptist. Elizabeth immediately recognized that God had chosen Mary for a special role. She called Mary the mother of the Lord, and pronounced a blessing on Mary. Mary must have been greatly reassured by Elizabeth's response to her arrival.

#7—MARY'S "MAGNIFICAT" (LUKE 1:46-56).

Having been received and reassured so remarkably by Elizabeth, Mary expressed her heart by glorifying, or magnifying, God in a song of praise. Because this song magnifies the greatness of God, it has been called Mary's "Magnificat." In this heartfelt song of praise, Mary extolled the greatness and holiness of God. She acknowledged God's great power, particularly as it related to the miraculous conception of Jesus in her womb. We can only imagine the kinds of conversations Mary and

Elizabeth enjoyed during their time together. But after three months it was time for Mary to return to Nazareth.

18—THE BIRTH OF JOHN THE BAPTIST (LUKE 1:57-66).

It was also time for Elizabeth to give birth to her son, John. Elizabeth's neighbors shared in her joy at the unusual birth of this unusual child. According to Jewish custom, the parents assigned a child's name on the eighth day after its birth, at the time when the ancient rite of circumcision was performed. When it came time to circumcise Elizabeth's son, everyone assumed that the child would be named after his father Zechariah. But Elizabeth insisted on naming the child John in obedience to Gabriel's command. Zechariah, still unable to speak, affirmed this decision by writing the child's name on a tablet. At that moment Zechariah was again enabled to speak. Bottled up for nine months, Zechariah's first words were expressions of praise to God. News spread, and the entire countryside heard about these remarkable events. People wondered what this child would accomplish. There was a hint of expectancy in the air. This child, John the Baptist, would in his adulthood burst onto the scene as a fiery prophet calling people to repentance and preparing people for the coming of their king, God's Messiah, Jesus.

19—ZECHARIAH'S PROPHECY (LUKE 1:67-80).

Now that Zechariah could once again speak, he opened his mouth with a prophetic declaration. Zechariah praised God for redeeming and saving His people. This act of redemption, this saving work of God would take place not many years later through Jesus Christ. It's interesting that Zechariah's prophetic song begins, not with his own son John, but with God's Son, Jesus. But then Zechariah refers to his own son, predicting that John would become a prophet of the Most High. John would lead the way, preparing people for the Lord's arrival. John's role would be both influential and monumental. God was beginning a new work among His people. John the Baptist would open the door for that new work, and in would walk Jesus Christ.

#10—THE ANNUNCIATION TO JOSEPH (MATTHEW 1:18-25).

By now Mary would have arrived back in Nazareth after her three-month visit with Elizabeth. Mary may have shown signs that she was going to have a baby. Although Mary was a virgin, she was pledged in marriage to a man named Joseph. Understandably, Joseph was deeply disturbed to discover that his promised bride was expecting a child. He could have disgraced Mary publicly, but because he was a devout man, Joseph's faith taught him to be gentle and gracious. He decided instead to privately cut his ties with Mary. Because of the marriage customs of that day, this required a legal divorce even though Joseph and Mary had never been together as husband and wife.

Then an angel appeared to Joseph in a dream. The angel told Joseph that Mary had been faithful, and that her child was the product of a miraculous work of God. He instructed Joseph to take Mary in as his wife and, when Mary's son was born, to name the child

Jesus. Matthew reminds us that the virgin birth of Jesus fulfilled Old Testament prophecies. God always keeps His promises. When Joseph woke up from his dream, he humbly and obediently took Mary home as his wife, sheltering her from disgrace and honoring her as the virgin mother of Jesus. Truly a remarkable man, Joseph fulfilled a unique role in the drama of the birth of Jesus Christ.

#11—THE BIRTH OF JESUS (LUKE 2:1-7).

Only Luke gives us the details of Jesus' birth, the Christmas story as it's come to be known. But those details are precious! It all took place during the reign of Caesar Augustus, ruler of the Roman Empire. Through God's providential direction, Augustus ordered a census throughout his expansive domain. As a result, people had to return to their ancestral homes to register in this census. Because Joseph was a descendant of David, he and Mary left Nazareth and went to David's hometown, Bethlehem. While they were in Bethlehem the time came for Mary's baby to be born. Bethlehem was apparently overcrowded at the time due to the requirements of the census, so Joseph and Mary had taken up the best lodging they could find. There, in a humble stable, Mary gave birth to a baby boy. There, Mary lovingly wrapped this child in the best bundling cloth she could provide. There, Mary placed her newborn son in a manger, the only cradle available in these humble surroundings. There lay her son, the Son of God, surrounded by love and humility and joy and curiosity. There lay Jesus.

12—THE VISIT BY THE SHEPHERDS (LUKE 2:8-20).

The night was already richly eventful. Jesus had been born. But God chose that His Son's birth should not go unnoticed. Therefore, He sent an angel to a field near Bethlehem. Shepherds were living out in these open fields, providing protection for their flocks of sheep. But that night these shepherds became the first recipients of the good news of Jesus' birth. The angel, surrounded by the radiance of God's glory, appeared to these shepherds. This heavenly messenger assured the shepherds that they need not be afraid. He had come to give them good news. The promised Savior, the Messiah or Christ, had been born that very night. Furthermore, that infant Savior was nearby. The angel invited the shepherds to go to the stable and find the baby lying in a manger. Then they would know that the angel's message was true. At that moment a multitude of angels appeared and proclaimed as only angels can the glory of God.

Once the angels had returned to heaven, the shepherds decided to go to Bethlehem and see this unusual sight. They believed that what the angel had announced was truly a message from God, and their faith drove them to respond. Of course, they were not disappointed. Just as the angel had declared, the shepherds found Mary and Joseph, along with a baby lying in a manger. These humble shepherds went out and spread the news about Jesus. Meanwhile, Mary continued to be amazed at the circumstances surrounding her life, her son, and her God. Truly, Jesus was and is unique. He is God and man in one. He is our Savior and our King.

Jesus' Infancy and Childhood

The four Gospels provide very little information about the childhood of Jesus, but they do relate some significant events that followed His birth. While we might wish for more information about the years leading up to Jesus' public ministry, we can rest assured that God has given us in His inspired Word everything we need to know to live like His Son.

#13—JESUS' CIRCUMCISION (LUKE 2:21).

As we saw with John the Baptist, it was customary for Jewish parents to circumcise their sons on the eighth day after their birth. Joseph and Mary, in full compliance with the commands of God, had Jesus circumcised. On that day they officially named Him Jesus in obedience to their angelic messenger. Jesus means Savior, and indeed Jesus would be our Savior and our Lord.

#14—JESUS' PRESENTATION IN THE TEMPLE (LUKE 2:22-24).

In addition to circumcision, Jewish law also required that parents consecrate their firstborn sons, that is, present their firstborn to the Lord for His purposes. This act of consecration took place at the same time that the mother was to present an offering at the Temple for her own purification. Mary and Joseph, still living in Bethlehem, made the six-mile journey to Jerusalem to perform these rites about forty days after Jesus' birth. There at the Temple, Mary presented her purification offering. Her offering, a pair of doves or pigeons, indicates that Mary and Joseph were considered to be among the poor in the land, since only the poor could present such meager offerings for purification. Although Mary and Joseph were poor in material possessions, they were rich in faith. Carrying the infant Jesus to the Temple must have been a joy for this devout couple. Incidentally, this was Jesus' first visit to the Temple, but it would not be His last! One day years later Jesus would march through that same Temple area, overturning the tables of moneychangers and upholding the holiness of worship. The Temple would indeed see Jesus again and again.

#15—SIMEON'S PROPHECY (LUKE 2:25-35).

While Mary and Joseph were at the Temple to perform the rites of purification and consecration they experienced two surprising encounters. Their first encounter was with a man named Simeon. Simeon was an elderly man whom God had promised would see the Messiah before his death. On the very day that Jesus was consecrated, the Holy Spirit of God moved Simeon to visit the Temple. There, Simeon saw Jesus. He took the baby in his arms and offered a prayer of praise to God for fulfilling His promise. Simeon had seen the Messiah, the One who would bring salvation to God's people. Simeon then reassured Mary that Jesus would accomplish great things for God, but also warned Mary that she would experience great pain in the process. In fact, Mary did later experience enormous pain. She saw her precious son nailed to a cross. This mother's amazement at Simeon's words would one day be surpassed by her agony, only to be surpassed once again by joy when Jesus would rise from the dead.

#16—ANNA'S PROPHECY (LUKE 2:36-38).

Mary and Joseph's second encounter in the Temple that day involved an elderly woman named Anna. Anna was a widow of many years. She frequented the Temple daily. At the very moment that Simeon took Jesus in his arms and announced his message to Mary, Anna arrived on the scene. She, too, gave praise to God and told the people present that this infant would bring redemption. Mary and Joseph must have been astounded by these encounters, and they must have taken great comfort in knowing that God was doing an unparalleled work through them. Jesus, their infant son, was the Son of God, the Messiah, the Savior and Redeemer.

#17—THE VISIT BY THE WISE MEN (MATTHEW 2:1-12).

After fulfilling their responsibilities at the Temple, Mary and Joseph would have returned to their temporary home in Bethlehem. But their lives would be anything but normal. They were soon to experience yet another unusual encounter. Magi from an eastern land would make a long journey to see Jesus, the King of the Jews. Although we often think of the wise men visiting Jesus in the stable, it makes more sense to place their arrival sometime after Jesus' consecration at the Temple. After all, shortly following the arrival of the magi, Mary and Joseph had to flee to Egypt for safety. Jerusalem and the Temple would be unsafe for their precious son.

Matthew's Gospel alone tells us about the magi from the east. Their identity is puzzling, but they were apparently scholars and astronomers to whom God graciously revealed the arrival of Jesus. The magi, guided by a star—possibly the radiant revelation of God's glory— journeyed to Jerusalem where they met with King Herod. Herod was a cruel man by every measure, as even secular history reveals. The magi informed Herod that a new King of the Jews had been born. Herod was threatened by any hint of challenge to his throne. He called together the religious scholars who informed him that the Scriptures pointed to Bethlehem as the birthplace of the Messiah. Herod sent the magi to Bethlehem to seek the child, feigning a personal desire to follow later and offer his own worship to this new king.

The magi left for Bethlehem, and the star appeared again to guide them to the house in which Mary, Joseph, and Jesus were living. There the magi presented the infant Jesus with costly gifts—gold, frankincense, and myrrh. Then God warned the magi in a dream not to return to Herod, so they avoided Jerusalem as they made their long journey home. Mary and Joseph must have once again been baffled by such an unusual visit, and this poor couple was greatly assisted by the gifts these magi brought.

#18—THE FLIGHT TO EGYPT (MATTHEW 2:13-15).

Little did Mary and Joseph know that their new financial resources would be needed so quickly. When the magi left, an angel appeared to Joseph and warned him to flee to Egypt. Herod, who had been duped by the magi and who jealously guarded his throne, would be eager to eliminate anyone identified as the new King of the Jews. Joseph obeyed immediately. In the middle of the night he, Mary, and Jesus began their flight to Egypt, where they stayed until Herod's death. By God's miraculous provision, Jesus was safe. His life was spared so that one day He could give His life as a ransom for us.

#19—THE SLAUGHTER OF THE INNOCENTS (MATTHEW 2:16-18).

Although Jesus had escaped Herod's hatred, Bethlehem suffered the evil rage of this rampant tyrant. As soon as it became apparent to Herod that the magi had outmaneuvered him, he ordered that all baby boys in Bethlehem under two years old be slaughtered. By this cruel method, Herod thought that he could eliminate any threat to his throne. Herod's extermination of these innocent children was but one of many crimes committed by this madman. To the people of Bethlehem this act of cruelty brought untold grief. Herod would soon die. His throne would be given to others, some as heartless as he. The people of God needed a king who would reign in righteousness. That King was alive, hidden away in Egypt.

#20—THE RETURN TO NAZARETH (MATTHEW 2:19-23; LUKE 2:39-40).

News reached Egypt that Herod was dead. In fact, an angel again appeared to Joseph and instructed him to return to the land of Israel. Jesus' life was no longer in jeopardy. Once again, Joseph obeyed the heavenly messenger and took Mary and Jesus back to Israel. However, because Herod's son now ruled over the southern region of Israel, Joseph didn't return to Bethlehem. Having been warned in a dream, Joseph chose instead to return to Nazareth in the northern region called Galilee. Nazareth was Mary and Joseph's hometown. Nazareth, that obscure village in Galilee, would be the place where Jesus would grow into manhood.

#21—JESUS IN THE TEMPLE AT AGE TWELVE (LUKE 2:41-50).

The silent years of Jesus' childhood are broken only by one account in the Gospel of Luke. Mary and Joseph consistently obeyed God's Word. They went annually to Jerusalem to celebrate the Passover, a feast commemorating God's work of rescuing the Israelites from slavery in Egypt. No doubt Jesus, as a boy, made this yearly journey with His parents. When Jesus was twelve years old He again made this journey to Jerusalem with Mary and Joseph, along with many others who would have traveled together to the feast. When Passover was finished, the band of travelers began their journey back to Galilee. Mary and Joseph assumed that Jesus was among their friends and relatives as they made their way north. But Jesus had remained behind.

Any parent knows the feeling, either real or imaginary, of losing a child in a crowd. When the caravan stopped for the evening, Mary and Joseph were distressed to discover that Jesus was nowhere to be found. Had they misplaced the Son of God? Of course, Mary and Joseph quickly returned to Jerusalem, where they found Jesus in the

Temple courts interacting with the scholars and scribes. Jesus was asking questions and posing answers of His own, answers that amazed those who heard Him. Mary, delighted and astonished, asked Jesus why He had stayed behind. Why had He put them through an emotional ringer? Jesus, in His first recorded words, simply and respectfully stated, "Why were you searching for me? Didn't you know that I had to be involved in the things of my Father?" In His earliest statement, Jesus declared His unique relationship with God the Father and His unique role in performing the Father's purposes for His life. Jesus knew as a child that He had a task to perform, one that set Him apart from all others. He would be devoted to accomplishing His heavenly Father's business.

1:22—Jesus' Growth and Human Development (Luke 2:51-52).

Obediently, Jesus went with Mary and Joseph back to Nazareth. He was truly an extraordinary child. Mary continually reflected on all the unique circumstances in her son's life. She must have thought often about the initial announcement by Gabriel that she, a virgin, would have a son. She would have turned over and over in her mind the fact that Elizabeth's son, John, while still in the womb leaped for joy at her arrival. She would have remembered Joseph's kindness that he attributed to an angelic message. Mary would have thought about the stable, the shepherds, Simeon and Anna in the Temple, the arrival of the magi, and now Jesus' amazing interaction with the religious scholars in the Temple. While she reflected, she cared for Jesus. Jesus, the Gospel of Luke tells us, grew mentally, physically, socially, and spiritually. We know that Jesus learned Joseph's skills, engaging in the work of carpentry. We know that Jesus was perfectly obedient to His parents and to the Law of God. We also know that Jesus would, as an adult, enter into a new phase of life. He would begin a public ministry in which He would heal the sick, help the poor, call God's people to repentance, and eventually die on a cross for our sins. But those days were yet ahead. For now, Jesus spent the bulk of His years simply growing up in Nazareth, growing up to fulfill the eternal plan of God.

2

THE EARLY JUDEAN AND SAMARIAN MINISTRY OF JESUS

SHORTLY AFTER THE BIRTH OF JESUS CHRIST, HEROD the Great, that tyrant king of the Jews, died. Although Herod had attempted to protect his throne, the Roman authorities divided his kingdom into several distinct regions. The southern region, called Judea, consisted of hills and deserts, with Jerusalem as its heart. East of Judea, beyond the Jordan River, was the land of Perea. North of Judea the central hill country was known as Samaria, with its mixed population of Jews and Gentiles who had intermarried generations earlier. North of Samaria was Galilee, including Nazareth, the Sea of Galilee, and the harbor village of Capernaum, which would each play such important roles in the life of Jesus Christ. Jesus grew up in Nazareth, in the northern region called Galilee. But He would carry on an itinerant ministry. This traveling ministry makes it possible for us to describe Jesus' life using geographic terms. Although

He grew up in Galilee, Jesus' public ministry began in the southern region of Judea where John the Baptist had begun his prophetic ministry.

Jesus' Initial Public Ministry

The story of Jesus' ministry begins with John the Baptist. God raised up John to be a powerful prophet and the forerunner of the Messiah. John's preaching prepared the hearts of many for the arrival of Jesus. In addition, it would be John's great privilege to introduce Jesus to the world.

#23—THE MINISTRY OF JOHN THE BAPTIST (MATTHEW 3:1-12; MARK 1:1-8; LUKE 3:1-20).

Luke's Gospel anchors the events of Jesus' ministry in its historical context. Tiberius was now the Roman emperor. Pontius Pilate had become the governor of Judea. Two descendants of Herod the Great ruled portions of the land, Herod Antipas having jurisdiction over Galilee and Perea, and Herod Philip ruling over the regions east of Galilee. Luke's historical note reminds us that the events of Jesus' life took place in time and space. He really lived, He really walked among us, He really died and rose again.

It was within this historical context that messianic expectations grew among the people of God. The Jews were ready for a change. They desperately wanted David's promised descendant to rule on the throne. At this very moment in history John the Baptist burst on the scene. The Old Testament scriptures had predicted such an individual, a "voice crying in the wilderness." Indeed,

John's ministry took place in the desert of Judea where he called God's people to repent. They had lived for themselves long enough. It was now time to turn back to God. John must have been a striking figure. He wore the traditional garb of the ancient prophets—a camel hair tunic and a leather belt. He lived and preached in the rugged Judean wilderness. He challenged people to demonstrate their repentance by being baptized in the Jordan River. Many people, hungry for spiritual reality, responded to John's message and were baptized.

Not everyone, however, was favorably impressed with John's message. Two sects of religious leaders, the legalistic Pharisees and the compromising Sadducees, went out to the Judean desert to inspect John's work. John addressed these skeptics in harsh terms, referring to them as snakes and demanding that they show fruit of repentance. At the same time John assured the crowds that he himself was not the Messiah they were anticipating. The Messiah would be more powerful, more authoritative, and more worthy of honor. In fact, John described himself as unworthy even to untie the coming Messiah's sandal! The Messiah would baptize, not with water, but with the Holy Spirit and fire.

24—THE BAPTISM OF JESUS (MATTHEW 3:13-17; MARK 1:9-11; LUKE 3:21-22).

One day while John was carrying out his prophetic ministry and baptizing converts in the Jordan River, Jesus arrived on the scene. He went to John to be baptized, not because He had any need to repent but so that He could be identified with John's message and ministry. Although they had likely never met, John recognized Jesus as the promised Messiah. He insisted that he was unworthy of baptizing Jesus, but Jesus persisted. So John baptized Jesus. At the moment that Jesus came up out of the waters of baptism, heaven was opened, the Holy Spirit in the form of a dove descended on Him, and a voice from heaven trumpeted, "This is my beloved Son, with whom I am well pleased." Here we see the triune God—the Father speaking from heaven, the Son submitting to baptism, and the Holy Spirit descending on Jesus. God was initiating a wonderful and powerful work on earth.

25—THE TEMPTATION OF JESUS (MATTHEW 4:1-11; MARK 1:12-13; LUKE 4:1-13).

Before Jesus could begin His powerful ministry among the people, it seems that He first had to display His power in the spiritual realm. Therefore, as Mark's Gospel tells us, the Holy Spirit sent Jesus out into the desert where the incarnate Son of God would face unparalleled temptation. Jesus fasted for forty days and, according to Luke's Gospel, Satan tempted Him throughout that entire forty day period. We read of only three specific temptations, but these may have been the final salvos launched by a desperate devil anxious to destroy the possibility of Jesus' redeeming work. Those three final temptations were, indeed, powerful enticements. But Jesus never flinched. Satan tempted Jesus to satisfy His human hunger by making bread out of stones. He tempted Jesus to test the Father's love by throwing Himself from a high point of the Temple. He tempted Jesus to avoid the cross and still rescue the kingdoms of the earth by bowing in worship to him. Jesus rejected each and every temptation, citing various scriptures as His weapon against Satan's enticements. Each time Jesus was tempted He said, "It is written." It is written that we cannot live on bread alone, that we must not test God's love, and that we dare not worship anyone or anything but God alone. Jesus proved Himself to be the holy Son of God by defeating Satan in the desert. Later, Jesus would defeat Satan at the cross. When this period of intense persecution came to an end, angels came to Jesus to attend to His needs. Now that Jesus had proven His power in the spiritual realm, He could freely minister to the physical and spiritual needs of God's people.

26—THE TESTIMONY OF JOHN THE BAPTIST ABOUT JESUS (JOHN 1:15-28).

While Jesus was in the Judean desert facing Satan's temptations, John the Baptist continued to carry out his prophetic work. He continued to testify to Jesus' identity as the long awaited Messiah and Savior. Some had assumed that John would be that Messiah, or that he was Elijah, or perhaps some other unique prophet who would assume a great role of leadership among God's people. John denied any such associations. He simply described himself as a voice in the desert who was preparing the way for the Lord. By referring to Jesus as "Lord," quoting from a prophecy in Isaiah 40:3 that referred to God, John was identifying Jesus as much more than a man. Jesus is God in the flesh. John continued to assure the people that Jesus, the One who would come after him, was by far the greater of the two.

#27—JOHN IDENTIFIES JESUS AS THE LAMB OF GOD (JOHN 1:29-34).

The day after one such encounter with those who questioned John, Jesus returned from His period of temptation in the desert. When John saw Jesus he declared, "Behold, the Lamb of God, who takes away the sin of the world." He identified Jesus as the One who was greater. In fact, John said that Jesus existed before he did. We know that John was born before Jesus, so John must have been referring to Jesus' pre-incarnate existence, His eternal deity. John recognized that Jesus is God, preexistent, eternal God. By John's own admission it was his privilege to reveal Jesus to the people of Israel. He testified how he had seen the Holy Spirit descend on Jesus at His baptism. God had previously informed John that the descent of the Holy Spirit would be a sign identifying the Messiah. John had no doubt. Jesus was the promised Messiah. He was the Lamb of God who would die for our sins. He is the Son of God who deserves our utmost reverence and worship.

#28—JESUS CALLS HIS FIRST DISCIPLES (JOHN 1:35-51).

John had impacted the lives of many people with his preaching. Some had joined him in his ministry, becoming his "disciples." A disciple is the student of a master teacher, an apprentice in the things of God. John had disciples, and Jesus, too, would gather a band of disciples to assist Him in His great work.

The day after Jesus had returned to John's place of baptism, John pointed Jesus out to two of his disciples, again describing Jesus as the Lamb of God. These two disciples of John, no doubt with John's blessing, began to follow Jesus. Jesus asked them what they wanted, and they simply asked where Jesus was staying, hinting that they wanted to become His disciples. Jesus openly invited them to follow, saying, "Come and see." They spent that entire day with Jesus.

One of these first two disciples of Jesus was a man named Andrew. Andrew had a brother named Simon. Andrew went to Simon and told him that he had found the Messiah. Andrew then brought Simon to see Jesus. Jesus took one look at Simon and gave him a new name, Peter. The Greek name Peter and its Aramaic equivalent, Cephas, mean Rock. Jesus saw in Peter someone who would be a rock, a foundation to His ministry. Peter's brother Andrew is often described as Jesus' first disciple. He is also famous for bringing people to Jesus. His first act as a disciple was to bring his own brother, Simon Peter, to the Lord. He serves as a model of evangelism for all Christians.

The next day Jesus decided to leave Judea and return to Galilee. Before beginning His journey, however, Jesus extended an invitation to a man named Philip to follow Him as a disciple. Philip was from Bethsaida, a town along the shore of the Sea of Galilee, as were Andrew and Peter. Philip went to another man, Nathanael, and told him that the promised Messiah had come. The promised Messiah was Jesus from Nazareth. Nathanael was skeptical. He doubted that the Messiah could hale from such an insignificant town such as Nazareth. But Philip pressed Nathanael to come with him and see Jesus. As Nathanael approached Jesus, without introduction Jesus declared that Nathanael was a man of true character. Nathanael, puzzled by this statement, asked how Jesus knew anything about him. Jesus said that He saw Nathanael under a fig tree before Philip spoke to him. Jesus, in His divine omniscience, knew all about Nathanael. Nathanael, impressed with this miraculous display of knowledge, declared that Jesus was the Son of God and the King of Israel. Jesus told Nathanael that he would witness many greater things than this display of His omniscience. He would see heaven opened before him and angels ascending and descending on Jesus.

Jesus' work in Judea was completed for the time being. He had been baptized by John. He had overcome intense temptation in the desert. He had been introduced to the world through John's witness. He had gathered an initial band of disciples. His followers included Andrew, Peter, Philip, Nathanael, and one other unnamed disciple. You'll remember that two of John the Baptist's disciples followed Jesus. One was Andrew. The other was not identified. But since John's Gospel alone records this event, and since John the disciple (not to be confused with John the Baptist) never mentions himself by name in his Gospel, it is likely that this other disciple was John. So Jesus, with His first five disciples, left Judea and returned to Galilee. It was in Galilee that Jesus would inaugurate His miraculous ministry.

1:29—JESUS CHANGES WATER INTO WINE (JOHN 2:1-12).

It is generally agreed that the first physical miracle that Jesus performed was turning water into wine. John's

Gospel describes this event as the beginning of Jesus' miraculous signs. It came about like this. There was a wedding in a small town near Nazareth called Cana. Jesus' mother, Mary, was one of the guests at this wedding celebration. Jesus, too, had been invited, along with His disciples. A wedding feast in ancient Israel wasn't just a one day event. It took the better part of a week. As the week wore on, the bridegroom's supply of wine ran out. Some have suggested that the last minute arrival of Jesus and His disciples contributed to the depletion of the banquet supplies. Possibly the host hadn't planned adequately, or the family was too poor to make better provisions. All we really know is that there was no more wine. This would have been a tremendous social embarrassment to the bridegroom and his family.

Mary went to Jesus and informed Him of the situation. Did she have some motherly sense that her son, the Son of God, would use this opportunity to reveal Himself to the world? Jesus responded to Mary by asking why she was involving Him in this situation. After all, His time to present Himself as God's Messiah hadn't yet arrived. It's always difficult to conjecture from the printed words alone the tone of voice or the facial expressions involved in such conversations. It's possible that Jesus, with a smile and knowing wink, responded to His mother in such a way that both knew what was about to take place. After all, Mary immediately told the servants to do anything Jesus asked.

We read that there were six large stone water jars nearby. Jesus asked the servants to fill these jars with water, which they did immediately. He then told the servants to draw some water from the jars and present it to the banquet host. We can only imagine what was going through the minds of these servants. Why would they present a cup of water to the host who had run short of wine? Was this some cruel joke? Nonetheless, the servants complied with Jesus' request. The host took the cup, not knowing where it came from, and tasted its contents. The cup was filled with wine, and not just any wine, but the best of wine! The host called the bridegroom aside and congratulated him on saving the best wine until the end. The wedding feast would now continue in style. Apart from Jesus and Mary, the servants and Jesus' disciples alone knew the source of this new wine. They must have been astounded. Jesus had performed a great miracle. He demonstrated His power over physical elements, transforming ordinary water into wine. But He did so privately, not seeking attention nor revealing Himself publicly to the crowd. That time would come soon enough. For now, Jesus used His miraculous power to honor His mother's request, to rescue a family from social embarrassment, to endorse forever the institution of marriage, and to reveal His glory to His disciples. John tells us that Jesus' disciples put their faith in Him as a result. They would again and again see Jesus perform miracles, and they would again and again grow in their belief in this Man who could turn water into wine.

When the wedding feast was over, Jesus, along with His disciples, His mother, and His brothers, left Cana and spent a few days in Capernaum, a fishing village along the shore of the Sea of Galilee. The Gospels indicate that

Jesus had brothers and sisters. He was part of a family, and He spent time with His family. We also know that some of Jesus' disciples were fishermen who had made Capernaum their base of operation. Jesus, too, would eventually make Capernaum His base of operation for His itinerant ministry. But for now, Jesus simply went to Capernaum to spend time with His family and friends. He would reveal Himself publicly, not in Galilee, but in Judea.

Jesus' Early Ministry in Judea

Jerusalem and its Temple, located in the southern region of Judea, was the heart of Judaism. You'll remember that every year Mary and Joseph took Jesus as a boy to Jerusalem in order to celebrate the Passover. As an adult, Jesus continued to make this annual journey. It was while Jesus was in Jerusalem to celebrate Passover that He publicly presented Himself as God's Messiah. He did so in a dramatic fashion.

AD30—THE FIRST CLEANSING OF THE TEMPLE (JOHN 2:13-25).

When Jesus arrived in Jerusalem for the Passover, He found the courtyards surrounding the Temple filled with merchants and moneychangers. After all, it would have been difficult for many of the Jews to transport a sacrificial animal from distant locations to Jerusalem for the Passover, so it had become common practice for merchants to make such animals available for purchase in Jerusalem.

In addition, these and other financial transactions invited the involvement of money changers, who likely inflated their prices for such events. That these practices took place was not really the problem. The problem was where they took place. The merchants and moneychangers had taken over the courts of the Temple for their transactions, making the place of worship a place for financial profit. This disregard for the holy place infuriated Jesus. John's Gospel tells us that He made a whip out of some rope and drove the animals out of the Temple area. Furthermore, He upended the tables of the moneychangers, sending coins flying everywhere. Like a fiery prophet of old, He zealously rebuked the merchants, accusing them of turning His Father's house into a marketplace. We must take note that in this dramatic and public inauguration of Jesus' ministry, He referred to the Temple as His own Father's house, highlighting His unique relationship with God the Father.

Of course, an act like this didn't go unchallenged. The Jewish leaders quickly accosted Jesus and asked Him by what authority He did these things. They demanded a sign of His authority. Jesus told them simply, "Destroy this temple, and I will raise it again in three days." The Jews were appalled. It had taken forty-six years to build this magnificent Temple in Jerusalem. Could Jesus really think He could do the same thing in three short days? They didn't realize that Jesus was talking about a different temple, His own body. Already Jesus knew that He would die and rise again on the third day. Already He knew that His ministry would be fraught with resistance. Instead of welcoming His cleansing of the Temple as they should, the religious leaders opposed this purifying act.

After purging the Temple, Jesus engaged in a ministry of miracles. John tells us that many people saw these miracles and believed in Him. Yet, John tells us, Jesus knew that their faith was fleeting in many cases. He didn't depend on the crowd because, as God in the flesh, He knew the makeup of the human heart. His ministry would draw crowds, but the crowds would one day turn against Him. Jesus knew that He had to change people one heart at a time.

#31—JESUS MEETS WITH NICODEMUS (JOHN 3:1-21).

One man who showed particular interest in Jesus was a Pharisee named Nicodemus. We must remember that the Pharisees, while often the archenemies of Jesus during His earthly ministry, were highly respected among the people. These were men of high regard, men who were committed to upholding the law of God in its finest detail. Many Pharisees, of course, took this commitment to the point of disregarding human needs and even disregarding the God they claimed to serve. But some were honest, thoughtful men seeking to know God's truth. Such was Nicodemus. Nicodemus would have been highly respected by the people because he was a Pharisee, and he was highly respected by the other religious and political leaders of Jerusalem to the degree that he had been appointed to the highest ruling council in the land.

Some have made great claims about Nicodemus' cowardice due to the fact that he went to Jesus at night, but such claims are far from necessary. The busyness of a man of Nicodemus' standing and the active ministry of Jesus may have made an evening meeting the best possible time for intimate discourse. We must give Nicodemus credit for seeking Jesus out. He respectfully called Jesus a teacher, or Rabbi, and stated that he and others believed that Jesus had been sent by God. After all, it would take a work of God to perform the kinds of miracles Jesus was doing.

Jesus cut to the heart of the matter. He told Nicodemus that, in order to see the kingdom of God, a person must be "reborn" or "born again." This statement seemingly caught Nicodemus off guard, and he asked Jesus how a person can experience a new birth. Surely this couldn't be a physical possibility. Jesus went on to explain that being reborn is a spiritual reality. We are born physically to enter into this world, but we must also be born spiritually to enter into God's kingdom. This spiritual rebirth is a work of the Spirit of God in a person's heart. It is a work of God that comes by faith. Jesus challenged Nicodemus to reflect on these spiritual realities. He also told Nicodemus that He alone, the Messianic Son of Man, had come from heaven and therefore was uniquely qualified to speak of heavenly truths. Jesus also said that He would one day be lifted up for all to see, speaking of the cross, and that anyone who would believe in Him would have eternal life.

It's in the context of Nicodemus' interview with Jesus that we find the most famous verse in the Bible, John 3:16. "For God so loved the world that He gave His only begotten Son, that whoever believes in Him shall not perish but have everlasting life." Faith in Jesus is the key to the new birth. Faith in Jesus is essential to entering into eternal life. Jesus brought spiritual light into a dark world. He shines His spotlight on our sin so that we might look to Him for forgiveness. We must believe in Jesus to be reborn, and we must be born again in order to enter His eternal kingdom. This is the lesson Jesus taught Nicodemus.

#32—JESUS MINISTERS AND BAPTIZES IN THE JUDEAN COUNTRYSIDE (JOHN 3:22-36).

Jesus and His disciples left Jerusalem, but instead of returning to Galilee they went out into the Judean countryside. There Jesus spent time with His disciples. This is significant. If we want to understand Jesus we have to spend time with Him. Jesus also engaged in a preaching and baptizing ministry similar to that of John the Baptist, although Jesus didn't actual baptize people, but left that work for His disciples to perform. In fact, John was still preaching and baptizing nearby. Some people went to John and told him that many people were abandoning his ministry and following Jesus instead. We might have expected John to become jealous of Jesus' popularity, but John was truly a man of God. He simply replied that he himself wasn't the Messiah. Jesus was the Messiah. Jesus must increase in popularity, while John indicated that he himself should decrease. The time had come for Jesus to take center stage in the unfolding spiritual drama of the ages. Only Jesus can grant eternal life. He alone must be the object of our faith.

Jesus' Ministry in Samaria

We can't be certain how long Jesus stayed in Judea during this first phase of His public ministry. We know it began in the spring, during the feast of Passover. In the account of the woman at the well, Jesus states that the harvest was four months away. This may mean that Jesus went through Samaria during the winter time, four months prior to the spring harvest. Therefore, Jesus may have spent several months in Jerusalem and the Judean countryside. The time came, however, for Jesus to return north to Galilee. He would do so by passing through the middle region of Samaria where He would carry on a brief ministry connected with a woman in the Samaritan town of Sychar.

#33—JESUS WITHDRAWS FROM JUDEA TO GALILEE (JOHN 4:1-3).

News of Jesus' growing popularity in Judea had reached the ears of the ever cautious Pharisees. They'd heard that Jesus was gaining even more followers than the extremely popular John the Baptist. Jesus learned of the Pharisee's concern, and decided it was time for Him to go back to Galilee. He certainly didn't leave Judea out of fear of the Pharisees. Instead, Jesus must have calculated that His ministry would prematurely encounter too many obstacles if He remained in Judea. There were many more people to reach and much more work to be done. He could best carry on His ministry in the north, in Galilee.

#34—JESUS MEETS THE WOMAN AT THE WELL (JOHN 4:4-42).

As Jesus and His disciples made their way north, they traveled through Samaria, stopping at the town of Sychar. This town was famous for its ancient connection with Jacob, the patriarch of the twelve tribes of Israel. Centuries earlier, Jacob had given this land with its valuable water source to his son, Joseph. Jacob's well was still in use in Jesus' day. When Jesus and His disciples arrived at Sychar, Jesus chose to remain alone beside the well outside of town. He sent His disciples into town to purchase supplies. Of course, Jesus knew that He would have an encounter with a spiritually thirsty woman beside that well.

A Samaritan woman soon arrived at Jacob's well. Jesus engaged her in conversation, asking her for a drink of water. She responded as one might expect from a race of people who were despised by most Jews. She asked Jesus how He, a Jew, dared speak with her, a Samaritan and a woman at that. Jesus wasn't at all taken aback by the woman's response. Instead, He continued the conversation, saying that He had the ability to provide for her something unique, living water. Of course, Jesus was speaking of spiritual things. But the woman was still focused on her physical needs. She asked how Jesus thought He might draw up living water from a deep well without a bucket and rope. Jesus reminded the woman that the water from Jacob's well would only quench her thirst temporarily. He could quench her spiritual thirst forever.

The offer of eternal life interested the woman, and

she asked Jesus to give her this living water. But first Jesus had to help the woman see her true need. He asked her to send for her husband, knowing that the woman had been married multiple times and was now living with a man to whom she was not married. When He stated this truth, the woman was surprised and said that she discerned that Jesus was a prophet. She posed a question to this prophet. Must people worship in Jerusalem as the Jews claimed, or could they worship God appropriately on the mountain at Sychar as the Samaritans did? Some see this question as a dodge, assuming the woman was trying to divert Jesus from the uncomfortable subject of her checkered past. But it makes more sense to consider the woman's question as a genuine reflection of her search for meaning in life. She truly wanted to know how she could connect with God.

Jesus assured the woman that a time was coming when the location of worship would matter nothing. After all, God seeks people of all races and places who will worship Him from the heart. The woman, intrigued by these statements, said that she believed the Messiah was coming and would be the one to explain all these things. Jesus then informed the woman that He Himself was the Messiah.

At this moment Jesus' disciples returned from town. They were surprised to see Jesus talking with a Samaritan woman. The woman left the well, leaving behind her water jar. Had her heart been fully satisfied with the living water that Jesus had offered to her through faith? The woman told the people in town that a man who could tell her everything she ever did was sitting at Jacob's well.

She suggested that this might be the Messiah. The people began to make their way to the well.

In the meantime Jesus' disciples encouraged Him to eat, but Jesus assured them that He was satisfied with the spiritual bread of accomplishing His Father's work. He then taught His disciples to look at people as a field ready for harvest. They were privileged to enter into a spiritual harvest, pointing people to eternal life.

Many of the people of Sychar put their faith in Jesus as the promised Messiah. They urged Jesus to stay with them, and Jesus remained in Sychar for two days. His teachings brought many more Samaritans to faith. They came to believe that Jesus is the Savior of the world. We, too, must come to see Jesus in this way. He is the Son of God, the Messiah, the Savior of the world. He alone can give us living water. He alone can grant us eternal life.

3

THE EARLY GALILEAN MINISTRY OF JESUS

JESUS DEVOTED A GREAT PROPORTION OF HIS TIME TO ministry in and around Galilee. This Great Galilean Ministry consisted of seven recorded preaching tours. It was interrupted briefly by two journeys to Jerusalem to celebrate the Jewish feasts. These two Jerusalem intermissions make it possible to neatly divide Jesus' Great Galilean Ministry into an early, middle, and late phase of work in this northern region. The Early Galilean Ministry probably took place from mid-winter until the Passover the following spring, a period of three or four months. This beginning of Jesus' work in Galilee consisted of His first two ministry tours, both of which concluded with events at Jesus' adopted home town of Capernaum.

Jesus' First Galilean Tour and Ministry at Capernaum

Galilee would prove to be both rewarding and challenging to Jesus' ministry. Many people flocked to Jesus in this early phase of His work. However, His own hometown would flatly reject Him. Delight and disappointment would follow Jesus throughout the hills of Galilee.

#35—JESUS' FIRST PREACHING TOUR OF GALILEE (LUKE 4:14-15; JOHN 4:43-45).

News about Jesus' ministry in Judea had spread north to the towns and villages of the Galilean district. In a brief summary statement, Luke tells us that it was "in the power of the Spirit" that Jesus made His return to His home region of Galilee, and that there Jesus taught in the synagogues throughout the countryside. According to John's Gospel, the people of Galilee welcomed Jesus warmly, having heard about and even personally witnessed some of His miraculous works in Jerusalem. But Jesus expressed His awareness that every prophet is without honor in his own country, and so anticipated resistance from those who knew Him best.

#36—JESUS HEALS A NOBLEMAN'S SON (JOHN 4:46-54).

Jesus' first miracle, turning water into wine, took place at Cana. Jesus returned to Cana early after His arrival back in Galilee. While Jesus was in Cana, a man came to Him from Capernaum seeking His help. This man, a nobleman or royal official, had a son who had become so ill that he was about to die. This nobleman went to Cana and begged Jesus to follow him back to Capernaum and heal his son. Jesus expressed His regret that people needed to see miraculous signs in order to believe in Him. No one yet could appreciate who Jesus was and what He could do. The nobleman continued to implore Jesus to go with him to Capernaum. Jesus simply replied that the man could go home on his own with the confidence that his son would live. Jesus didn't need to be physically present to procure the sick son's healing. The nobleman believed Jesus even without seeing the sign performed, which must have been a delight to Jesus. As the man was making his way back to Capernaum, his servants met him with the news that the boy had recovered. The nobleman inquired about the time of the boy's healing. The servants identified the precise day and hour, and this time coincided precisely with Jesus' declaration that the boy would live. The nobleman along with the members of his whole household put their faith in Jesus as a result of this miracle. John mentions that this was the second miracle that Jesus performed in the region of Galilee. More miracles would come, but first Jesus had to reveal Himself as God's Messiah in His hometown of Nazareth.

37—JESUS IS REJECTED AT NAZARETH (LUKE 4:16-30).

Jesus faithfully attended services in the synagogues each Sabbath day. When Jesus returned to Nazareth, He went to the synagogue and was invited to read the Scriptures. He turned to a passage in Isaiah that predicted the presence of the Holy Spirit in the life of the promised Messiah. The Messiah would preach good news to the poor, proclaim freedom to those in bondage, restore sight to the blind, relieve the oppressed, and proclaim the arrival of God's blessing and favor. Having read this messianic prophecy, Jesus rolled up the scroll, sat down, and declared that Isaiah's prediction was that day fulfilled. Jesus spoke, of course, of Himself as the promised Messiah. All eyes were glued on Jesus as He made this bold declaration. Luke's Gospel tells us that everyone spoke well of Jesus, amazed at the graciousness of His words. They were all the more impressed because they knew that Jesus was Joseph's son, the member of a local family. How had Jesus become so skillful in speaking? What did He mean by saying that Isaiah's prophecy had been fulfilled that day?

Jesus went on to say that He fully expected the people of Nazareth to demand a miraculous sign similar to that performed in Capernaum, presumably referring to the healing of the nobleman's son. Jesus also stated that no prophet is accepted in his own hometown. He gave the Old Testament prophets Elijah and Elisha as examples. During a period of intense famine, Elijah was rejected in Israel. Therefore, God sent Elijah to a widow in the Gentile region of Sidon. Elisha likewise experienced little acceptance by his own people, but healed a Gentile leper from Syria. These examples and their implications infuriated the people of Nazareth. They were so incensed by Jesus' statements that they actually drove Him out of town to one of the many precipices on which the village sat and attempted to throw Jesus to His death.

But then, at the moment of greatest danger, Jesus simply and miraculously turned around, walked through the middle of the mob, and left Nazareth behind. How His heart must have ached for these people who were so near to Him in His upbringing and who now would have nothing to do with His ministry of proclaiming God's good news! Jesus would not force Himself upon people. He would go where He was welcome.

AD 38—JESUS MOVES TO CAPERNAUM (MATTHEW 4:12-17; MARK 1:14-15; LUKE 4:31-32).

Jesus chose as His newly adopted home base the fishing village of Capernaum. One can't fault Jesus for making His home along the shores of the beautiful Sea of Galilee. Its peaceful waters would have provided multiple opportunities for Jesus to enjoy times of quiet prayer and reflection. Its waters, not always peaceful, would also provide a stage for some of Jesus' most dramatic miracles.

While Luke informs us that Jesus left Judea for Galilee in the power of the Holy Spirit, Matthew and Mark tell us that Jesus had also been prompted to leave Judea because John the Baptist had been imprisoned. Again, Jesus hadn't left Judea out of fear, but out of a sense of divine leading that would extend and expand His ministry until the time was right for His death. Jesus had a message to proclaim— the good news that God's promised kingdom was near. Like John the Baptist, Jesus called people to repent. Only by turning back to God would the people be prepared to receive God's imminent kingdom. This kingdom of God was, of course, identified with the person and work of Jesus Christ.

39—JESUS CALLS FOUR DISCIPLES (MATTHEW 4:18-22; MARK 1:16-20; LUKE 5:1-11).

As we have already seen, during His early Judean ministry Jesus had enlisted a handful of disciples to follow Him. This seems to have been a temporary commitment, appropriate to the opening months of Jesus' ministry. However, it now came time for Jesus to expect a lasting commitment from His followers. Three of Jesus' initial disciples—Andrew, Peter, and John—were fishermen who worked out of the village of Capernaum, Jesus' newly adopted home base. It certainly wasn't by accident that Jesus chose Capernaum as the base of His ministry operations. In addition to its beautiful location along the shore of the Sea of Galilee, Capernaum also provided personal contacts for Jesus' growing work.

One day as Jesus was walking along the shore He saw Peter and Andrew casting their fishing nets into the water. The long night of fishing was coming to an end, and apparently these two brothers were hoping for a final catch of fish. Unsuccessful in their efforts, they returned to shore and began washing their fishing nets to prepare them for their next fishing expedition. As usual, a crowd had gathered around Jesus as He was walking along. Eventually the crowd grew too large for Him to teach adequately while He walked, so Jesus stepped into one of the boats, the one belonging to Peter, and asked Peter to take Him a short distance off shore. Peter willingly complied, and Jesus taught the crowd from the vantage point of the fishing boat.

At the end of His discourse, Jesus instructed Peter to sail out into deeper water and let down the nets. Peter objected, saying that they had been fishing all night with no success. This seasoned fisherman knew that the fish just weren't "biting" that day. But out of respect for Jesus, Peter obeyed. Much to Peter's surprise, the nets were filled with fish, so full in fact that the nets began to tear! Peter quickly signaled for help, and his partners brought the other boat from shore. Both boats were filled with fish and nearly sank under the load. We can only imagine the flurry of activity on the part of these fishermen and the knowing, joyful laughter that must have burst from Jesus' mouth as He watched this event unfold.

Once back on shore, Peter fell to his knees in front of Jesus. He admitted that he was but a sinful man, unworthy to be in the presence of someone so great. But Jesus saw something different in Peter's heart. He said to Peter and his brother Andrew, "Don't be afraid. For now on you'll fish for men." Securing their boats on shore, Peter and Andrew unhesitatingly followed Jesus. Jesus then extended the same invitation to two other brothers, James and John. These two young men were working in their fishing boat with their father Zebedee along with some hired men. James and John immediately left their fishing trade and their father, doubtless with his blessing, and followed Jesus. These men would form the nucleus of a committed band of disciples whose lives would never be the same, whose lives would be instrumental in taking the good news of Jesus into a needy world.

#40—JESUS CASTS OUT A DEMON IN THE SYNAGOGUE (MARK 1:21-28; LUKE 4:33-37).

When the Sabbath day arrived, Jesus went as usual to the synagogue. There He taught the people the truths of God. He did so with such authority that the people expressed their amazement. On that particular Sabbath day there was a man in the synagogue who was possessed by an evil spirit. Jesus would frequently encounter demonic forces during His ministry. The spirit world is real, but Jesus' power far surpasses that of any demon or even Satan himself. After all, Jesus is the Son of God.

From down inside this unfortunate man, the demon cried out in a loud voice, "What do you want with us, Jesus of Nazareth?" The demon expressed deep fear of being cast into eternal judgment and acknowledged Jesus as "the Holy One of God." The spirit world recognizes Jesus' authority and trembles! Jesus commanded the demon to be quiet and come out of the man. The demon threw the man to the ground, though unable to injure him. It then came out of the man in submission to Jesus' authority.

The onlookers in the synagogue that day were again amazed at Jesus. Not only did He teach with authority, but He had the authority to command evil spirits and they were forced to obey Him. As a result, word about Jesus spread even more quickly throughout the region of Galilee.

41—JESUS HEALS PETER'S MOTHER-IN-LAW (MATTHEW 8:14-17; MARK 1:29-34; LUKE 4:38-41).

After Jesus left the synagogue He, along with James and John, went to the home of Peter and Andrew. When they arrived they discovered that Peter's mother-in-law was sick, lying in bed with a dangerously high fever. The members of her family asked Jesus to intervene. Jesus verbally rebuked the fever, took the sick woman's hand, and helped her to her feet. Instantly the fever was gone and Peter's mother-in-law was again in perfect health. She was able to go about her normal, joyful activities of taking care of her family and guests. Jesus' miraculous touch brought instant healing.

As evening approached, people began to bring to Jesus many sick friends and relatives. They also brought those who were demon possessed, having heard about the events in the synagogue earlier that day. Mark's Gospel tells us that the whole town gathered at the door of the house that evening. Jesus cast out demons and healed the sick. He met the needs of everyone who came to Him that evening. His first Galilean tour, which began in Cana and saw inexplicable rejection in Nazareth, ended with a great display of authoritative teaching and miraculous healings in Capernaum. In addition, Jesus now had four committed disciples who had forsaken their fishing careers to follow Him.

Jesus Second Galilean Tour and Ministry at Capernaum

Although Jesus had built a strong following in Capernaum, He wanted to take the good news of God's kingdom throughout many other towns and villages of Galilee. Thus began Jesus' second preaching tour.

₱42—JESUS' SECOND PREACHING TOUR OF GALILEE (MATTHEW 4:23-25; MARK 1:35-39; LUKE 4:42-44).

In one day Jesus had cast a demon out of a man in the synagogue, healed Peter's mother-in-law, and met the physical and spiritual needs of countless people in Capernaum. It had been a busy day, to say the least. Nonetheless, Jesus got up very early the next morning and went off to a solitary place to pray. This quiet time with His heavenly Father would be a hallmark of Jesus' ministry. When the people of Capernaum woke up they, along with the disciples, began to look for Jesus. When they found Him, they tried to convince Him to stay in Capernaum. But Jesus had other plans. He told His disciples that He had come to proclaim the good news throughout Galilee. This He did, teaching in the synagogues, healing the sick, and driving out demons from town to town. As Jesus did so, His notoriety spread well beyond the borders of Galilee. People from a much wider region began to bring their sick friends and family members to Jesus. Jesus now had a large following of people. But Jesus was still interested in the individual. He still cared for the needs of each person, especially the spiritual needs of the heart.

₱43—JESUS HEALS A LEPER (MATTHEW 8:1-4; MARK 1:40-45; LUKE 5:12-16).

One individual whose life Jesus touched was a man who suffered from the dreaded illness of leprosy. A leper was a social outcast by virtue of the spreading nature of this debilitating disease. One day a man inflicted with leprosy came and knelt before Jesus. He expressed his faith in Jesus' healing power and his respect for Jesus' will. If Jesus so desired, He could heal this man of his leprosy. Jesus touched the leprous man, a touch of healing that must have penetrated deep into this hurting man's very soul. After all, who would touch a leper? But Jesus touched the man and declared, "I am willing. Be clean!" The man was instantly cured of his leprosy.

Jesus then instructed the man not to tell anyone else about this healing. Instead, the man was to go to the priest and offer sacrificial gifts as the Law of Moses commanded. This act of sacrifice would appropriately serve as a testimony to the priests that God was at work. The man, however, began to tell everyone about how Jesus had healed him of his leprosy. Consequently, the crowds grew and Jesus couldn't travel as freely from town to town. Even in remote areas, people thronged Jesus seeking His healing power.

#44—JESUS HEALS A PARALYTIC MAN LET DOWN THROUGH A ROOF (MATTHEW 9:1-8; MARK 2:1-12; LUKE 5:17-26).

Eventually Jesus completed His second preaching tour of Galilee and returned to the seaside village of Capernaum. Once again many people gathered at the house where Jesus was staying. He gladly proclaimed God's truth to these crowds. The house was so full and the crowd outside so large that there was no way for anyone else to even get close to Jesus. Yet, one man desperately needed to see Jesus. He was a paralytic, and wanted to be healed. But how could a paralytic get near to Jesus?

Fortunately, this man had friends who helped him get to the house where Jesus was teaching. These friends were determined to bring the paralytic man to the feet of Jesus. Four of these friends picked the man up, carried him to the rooftop of the house, pulled back some of the tiles, and lowered their paralytic friend right in front of Jesus!

When Jesus saw their faith, He was impressed and declared to the paralytic man, "Your sins are forgiven." Jesus wasn't implying that the paralytic man's condition was a result of sin, but that the man's deepest need was spiritual instead of physical. The man had come to have his body healed, but Jesus first healed his soul.

Among the crowd that day were a number of religious leaders. These men took offense at Jesus' declaration of forgiveness. After all, only God can forgive sins. Who did Jesus think He was, declaring that this paralytic man's sins were forgiven? Jesus knew what these religious leaders were thinking. So He asked them which would be easier, to forgive sins or to tell a paralytic man to get up and walk. Of course, both would require the power and authority of God. Then Jesus demonstrated His divine authority by saying to the paralytic man, "Get up, pick up your mat, and go home." Immediately the man was healed. He stood up, picked up his mat, and praising God, left the house and headed for home. There had been no room for the man to enter the house, but it would have been fascinating to see how the crowd made room for him to walk out! This man had been touched by Jesus Christ. Once again the crowd was awestruck at Jesus' miraculous power.

#45—JESUS CALLS MATTHEW (MATTHEW 9:9-13; MARK 2:13-17; LUKE 5:27-32).

One day Jesus was walking along, teaching those who had gathered around Him. The town of Capernaum was situated at a crossroads of commerce, a prime location for the authorities to set up a station for collecting taxes from travelers. Tax collectors were generally despised by the people not simply because they gathered taxes but because they were often seen as dishonest in their dealings and as collaborators with the Roman government. One such tax collector was a man named Levi, also known to us as Matthew. As Jesus passed by the tax collector's booth, He turned to Matthew and simply said, "Follow me." Jesus was inviting Matthew to give up his trade and follow Him as a disciple. Wisely, Matthew left his lucrative career and followed Jesus. In addition to four fishermen, Jesus now had a tax collector as a disciple.

Matthew held a banquet in honor of Jesus. Many of Matthew's guests were other tax collectors and business associates considered to be sinners in the eyes of the common populace. This banquet didn't go unnoticed by the religious elite. The Pharisees asked the disciples why Jesus associated with tax collectors and sinners. Jesus responded to this question as only Jesus could. He said that only sick people need a doctor. These tax collectors and so-called sinners recognized that they had a spiritual need, and therefore welcomed Jesus as their spiritual doctor. Jesus had come to call sinners, not the righteous, to repentance. Of course, the Pharisees also needed what Jesus offered, but they were unwilling to admit their spiritual poverty. Therefore, they refused to repent and receive the forgiving grace of Jesus.

46—JESUS GIVES HIS PARABLES OF THE UN-SHRUNK CLOTH AND THE NEW WINESKINS (MATTHEW 9:14-17; MARK 2:18-22; LUKE 5:33-39).

At this time some of the disciples of John the Baptist came to Jesus with a question. We recall that John had been imprisoned for his preaching. John's followers had apparently spread out, and some were closely observing Jesus and His ministry. So, some of these disciples of John asked Jesus about ritual fasting. Why did John's disciples and the Pharisees' disciples engage in fasting, while Jesus and His disciples engaged in feasting? Matthew's banquet honoring Jesus probably sparked this question.

Jesus answered by describing Himself as a bridegroom and His disciples as friends of the bridegroom. At a wedding, everyone celebrates. Everyone feasts. While Jesus was present, His disciples should celebrate. But a time would come when Jesus would be taken away from His disciples. He would be crucified, and eventually return to heaven. At that time the disciples would find it appropriate to fast. Jesus knew that His ministry on earth would involve painful suffering. He knew that His followers would also suffer hardship and persecution for His sake. These realities were never far from Jesus' mind. But for the present, while Jesus was among them, it was appropriate for the disciples to celebrate joyfully the presence of their Messiah.

Jesus then presented a parable, the first recorded parable in Jesus' teaching ministry. A parable, simply stated, is a story about everyday life that illuminates eternal truths. Jesus described His message, the good news about God's kingdom, as something new and fresh that replaces that which is old and worn out. For example, you can't try to mend old clothes with new, un-shrunk cloth. The new cloth will soon tear away the stitches. Likewise, new wine can't be contained in old wineskins. Before glass bottles were invented, wine was made in the sown hides of animals. New wineskins were elastic, capable of expanding with the wine. But an old wineskin was brittle and wouldn't be able to accommodate fresh wine. Jesus said that His message and ministry were new. The old forms of approaching God had run their course. Now, Jesus was the way to the Father. Therefore, we should celebrate the presence, the power, and the redeeming work of Jesus Christ. Jesus is the new and living way. He is the only way. This parable brings to a conclusion the Early Galilean Ministry of Jesus.

4

THE MIDDLE GALILEAN
MINISTRY OF JESUS (PART 1)

DURING HIS EARLY GALILEAN MINISTRY, JESUS had engaged in two preaching tours. During that time He was rejected at Nazareth, He relocated His ministry to Capernaum, He called at least five committed disciples, He healed and helped countless people, and He proclaimed the good news of God's coming kingdom. His extended ministry in Galilee was interrupted briefly while Jesus attended one of the Jewish feasts in Jerusalem. He then returned to pursue the second phase of His ministry in Galilee known as the Middle Galilean Ministry.

Jesus' Third Galilean Tour and His Rejection by the Unrepentant Cities

Jesus' Middle Galilean Ministry would last about one year. During these months Jesus would engage in three more preaching tours, and, in spite of His miracles, experience increased opposition and outright rejection.

#47—JESUS HEALS A LAME MAN AT THE POOL OF BETHESDA (JOHN 5:1-47).

John's Gospel tells us that Jesus went back to Jerusalem to celebrate one of the Jewish feasts, but doesn't identify which feast. Many have assumed that this particular feast was the Jewish Passover, one of four Passover feasts during Jesus' public ministry. Based on this assumption, Jesus' ministry would have spanned a total of about three and one-half years. His Early Galilean Ministry would have lasted for about three or four months, from winter until spring. His Middle Galilean Ministry would have been one full year in duration, from one spring Passover to the next Passover. However, even if the unnamed feast in John's Gospel wasn't the Passover, Jesus' ministry could have still lasted a little over three years. The exact length of time involved in Jesus' public ministry isn't, of course, as important as what He accomplished during this time.

The only recorded event during Jesus' presumably short visit to Jerusalem on this occasion took place near one of the city's water reservoirs called the Pool of Bethesda. Because this pool was surrounded by several covered porches and because certain superstitions had risen about the healing qualities of this pool, many disabled people gathered around its waters. Many of these people believed that when the water in the pool stirred, the first one who would enter the water would be healed.

One man who sat beside the Pool of Bethesda caught Jesus' attention. This man was an invalid who had suffered in this condition of immobility for thirty-eight years. Jesus approached this man with a seemingly obvious question. He asked this poor invalid, "Do you want to be healed?" But Jesus' question pushed beyond the obvious. The real question was whether or not this man would seek healing, not from some superstition but from the supernatural touch of the Son of God.

The invalid responded to Jesus by saying that he did indeed want to be healed, but was unable to enter the pool's healing water before someone else took advantage of its mysterious effects. Jesus then said to this unfortunate man, "Get up, take your mat, and walk." Instantly the man was healed by Jesus' miraculous power.

This incident of healing the invalid beside the Pool of Bethesda should have been a matter of unparalleled joy. However, because Jesus healed this man on the Sabbath day, the religious leaders in Jerusalem took offense. They saw the former invalid carrying his mat as he had been instructed by Jesus and they rebuked him for this supposed violation of Sabbath law. The man simply replied that he had been instructed to do so by the one who had healed him. This former invalid didn't even know Jesus' name, but he knew that someone had performed a miracle in his life.

Later that day Jesus again encountered the former invalid. This time Jesus instructed the man to take stock of his life. He was to give up his sins. Jesus was always interested in the spiritual aspect of life, not just physical needs. The former invalid went back to the Jewish leaders to tell them that it was Jesus who had healed him. He probably intended to do Jesus a favor in this way, but the Jewish leaders weren't really interested in Jesus' message. Instead, they opposed Jesus for healing a man on the Sabbath day. In addition, because Jesus identified His work as the very work of His heavenly Father, the Jewish leaders began to look for a way to kill Jesus. After all, as they clearly recognized, Jesus was declaring Himself to be equal with God.

Jesus upheld His claim to deity, explaining to His opponents that He stood in a unique relationship to God the Father. Jesus claimed to have the right to judge and the power to grant life. He could even raise the dead. Nevertheless, Jesus would operate only in unison with His heavenly Father. He instructed the religious leaders to reflect on His endorsement by John the Baptist, to look at His miraculous works, and to examine what the Scriptures predicted about Him. He then accused His opponents of failing to receive God's love and therefore failing to receive Him, God's promised Messiah. Resistance to Jesus, His message, and His ministry was clearly growing in Jerusalem, and it would grow in Galilee as well.

48—JESUS DEFENDS HIS DISCIPLES FOR PLUCKING GRAIN ON THE SABBATH (MATTHEW 12:1-8; MARK 2:23-28; LUKE 6:1-5).

While Jesus and His disciples were returning from Jerusalem to Galilee, or possibly after they had arrived back in Galilee, they found themselves walking through a field of standing grain. The fact that the grain was ripe implies that it was nearly time for the spring harvest. As they walked through the grain field, Jesus' disciples innocently plucked some heads of grain, rubbed them between their hands to release the kernels, and popped the grain into their mouths to satisfy their appetite. However, because this took place on a Sabbath day, the ever-present Pharisees accused Jesus' disciples of violating Sabbath law. The Pharisees saw in the disciples' actions the work of harvesting.

Jesus defended His disciples, and thereby clarified the nature of the Sabbath day. He reminded the Pharisees that King David had once eaten consecrated bread to satisfy his hunger even though such bread was reserved for the priests. God's law was never intended to harm, but to help God's people. In addition, Jesus pointed out that the priests work on the Sabbath in order to fulfill their priestly functions. Jesus drove home His point by stating that God desires mercy. The Pharisees knew only law. They failed to show mercy toward others. But God is a God of mercy. In addition, Jesus declared that He, the Son of Man, is Lord of the Sabbath. He alone has authority to determine what should and shouldn't be done every day of our lives. He is truly Lord, even Lord of the Sabbath.

<u>49—JESUS HEALS A MAN WITH A SHRIVELED HAND (MATTHEW 12:9-14; MARK 3:1-6; LUKE 6:6-11).</u>

Jesus continued to experience conflicts from His opponents regarding Sabbath regulations. On one Sabbath day, Jesus went into the synagogue as was His custom. In that particular synagogue was a man who had a shriveled hand. The religious leaders, looking for an excuse to accuse Jesus, asked Him whether or not it was proper to heal someone on the Sabbath. Without hesitation Jesus invited the man with the shriveled hand to step forward. He told the audience that it was always appropriate to perform good deeds on the Sabbath. After all, everyone would rescue a domestic animal from danger even on the Sabbath day. Aren't people more valuable than animals? Then Jesus told the unfortunate man to stretch out his withered hand. As the man did so, his hand was immediately restored. The religious leaders could take this affront to their legalistic approach to God no longer. Their resistance turned to hatred, and they began to plot among themselves and with other influential people how they might put Jesus to death.

50—JESUS HEALS THE MULTITUDES (MATTHEW 12:15-21; MARK 3:7-12).

While many of the religious elite resisted Jesus, the multitudes still sought His miraculous healing touch. Jesus returned to the area around the Sea of Galilee, and an ever growing crowd followed Him. Mark's Gospel tells us that people from as far away as Judea and Idumea in the far south and Tyre and Sidon in the far north pursued Jesus. Jesus healed countless individuals and cast out countless demons. The sick flocked to Jesus and, because the crowd became so unwieldy, Jesus instructed His disciples to prepare a small boat so that He could retreat safely from the crowd. His ministry would include healing the sick, but could not be limited to these physical needs. Jesus must, as Isaiah the prophet had predicted, proclaim and promote justice among God's people. But He would do so in gentleness and compassion.

#51—JESUS CHOOSES HIS TWELVE APOSTLES (MARK 3:13-19; LUKE 6:12-16).

As we have seen, Jesus frequently sought times of solitude to pray. On one such occasion, Jesus spent a whole night in prayer somewhere in the hills surrounding the Sea of Galilee. The next morning, Jesus called His closest followers and chose twelve of them to be His specially appointed apostles. An apostle is someone who is sent with authority on behalf of another. These twelve apostles, whom we often refer to as the twelve disciples, received a special commission from Jesus. They would spend intimate time with Jesus, receiving special training for their role. Jesus granted them authority to preach and to cast out demons, fully replicating His own powerful ministry. We've already met six of these twelve apostles—Simon Peter, Andrew, James, John, Philip, and Matthew. The other six apostles were Bartholomew, Thomas, another man by the name of James, Simon who was a political zealot, and two men by the name of Judas, one of whom would later prove to be a traitor. These twelve apostles, excluding Judas Iscariot, would be so transformed by Jesus that they would one day revolutionize the world.

152—JESUS DELIVERS HIS SERMON ON THE MOUNT (MATTHEW 5:1—7:29; LUKE 6:17-49).

Although Jesus gave concentrated attention to His twelve disciples, He continued to invest time in the crowds of people who followed Him. On one such occasion Jesus delivered what has come to be known as His famous Sermon on the Mount. Both Matthew and Luke record this message. While these two Gospel writers may be recording similar messages delivered at separate times, it makes sense to see their two accounts as complementary reports of the same event.

The crowds had once again gathered around Jesus. He led them up on one of the hillsides overlooking the Sea of Galilee and began to teach. His message began with the Beatitudes. Jesus declared that God's blessing rested on those who are poor in spirit, who mourn, who are meek, and who are merciful. God honors those who hunger and thirst for righteousness, who demonstrate purity in their lives, and who uphold peace. Jesus also declared that God blesses those who are persecuted. All such people are to rejoice because God will richly reward them in heaven. After all, Jesus said, such men and women are the salt of the earth and the light of the world.

Jesus then went on to contrast the mere outward obedience to the law with the true meaning of doing God's will from the heart. Jesus wasn't abandoning God's law, but expanding on its application. For example, it isn't simply enough to refrain from murder. We must give up personal animosity and hatred toward one another. It isn't enough to refrain from acts of adultery. We must keep our hearts and minds pure from lustful thoughts. Instead of simply loving our neighbor, we're also to love our enemies. The way of Jesus Christ is far more demanding than the way of legalistic obedience, but it's also much more rewarding.

In this Sermon on the Mount, Jesus also gave His followers instructions on how to pray. Here we find recorded what we refer to as the Lord's Prayer, a model for us to build on as we pray to God. We're invited to address God as our heavenly Father, to acknowledge His holy character, and to request from Him our daily bread. Our prayers should also include confession of sin and an acknowledgement of God's kingdom rule.

The Sermon on the Mount also includes Jesus' teaching on laying up treasure in heaven, resisting the urge to worry about the simplest necessities of life, and refraining from treating others judgmentally. Here we also read some of Jesus' most famous words. For example, Jesus said, "But seek first God's kingdom and his righteousness." He warned about avoiding the broad path and instead taking the narrow road that leads to life. He also declared in very positive terms His Golden Rule: "Do unto others what you would have others do unto you." Those who had gathered on the hillside that day and heard Jesus deliver the Sermon on the Mount were treated to one of the most masterful messages of all time. They were also challenged to live as they had never lived before. Such was the message of Jesus that day, and such is His message today.

353—JESUS HEALS A CENTURION'S SERVANT (MATTHEW 8:5-13; LUKE 7:1-10).

Jesus returned to the village of Capernaum. There a centurion, a Roman military leader, came to Jesus for help. This rough and ready soldier had a tender heart toward the Jewish people. He also had a compassionate heart toward one of his servants who was sick and nearing death. Jesus assured the centurion that He would go and heal the dying servant. But then the centurion said something unusual. He explained to Jesus that, as a Roman military leader, he understood authority structures and was accustomed to seeing his spoken orders carried out. The centurion then said that he did not deserve to have someone of Jesus' authority come into his home. Instead, he acknowledged deep respect for Jesus' power to simply speak the word and the servant would be healed. Jesus was deeply impressed with this humble centurion's show of faith and dismissed the man with the assurance that the ailing servant would be restored. Indeed, when the centurion arrived at home his servant was completely healed.

354—JESUS RAISES A WIDOW'S SON FROM THE DEAD (LUKE 7:11-17).

The village of Nain rested in the hills of Galilee not far from Nazareth. This little village would witness one of Jesus' greatest miracles. Shortly after healing the centurion's servant in Capernaum, Jesus, along with His disciples, traveled the winding pathways to Nain. A large crowd continued to follow Him. As Jesus approached the village gate a funeral procession was emerging. The only son of a widowed mother had died and was being carried out for burial. The whole town seemed to be following the weeping mother. This mournful scene touched Jesus' heart deeply. He approached the dead son's coffin and, touching it, commanded the young man to get up. The dead son immediately sat up and began to talk. Jesus had raised him from the dead! Everyone was amazed at Jesus' resurrection power. They readily acknowledged that Jesus was a great prophet whom God had sent to help them. They did not yet realize that Jesus was much more than a prophet. He had power to raise the dead because He is the Son of God.

55—JOHN THE BAPTIST QUESTIONS JESUS (MATTHEW 11:2-6; LUKE 7:18-23).

While Jesus had been ministering throughout Galilee, His forerunner, John the Baptist, had been confined in prison. As the months wore on, this fiery prophet apparently began to have doubts about his ministry and his identification of Jesus as the long awaited Messiah. Such doubts are understandable given John's unjust imprisonment. When some of John's faithful disciples reported to him the mighty works that Jesus was performing, he sent two of them to ask Jesus to confirm His messianic identity. When these two messengers arrived where Jesus was working and asked Him John's question, Jesus performed a number of miracles in their presence. He healed the sick, cast out evil spirits, and restored sight to the blind. Then Jesus told John's disciples to return to John and describe the ministry they had seen

Him perform. In addition, Jesus told these messengers to reassure John that the good news of God's kingdom was still being proclaimed. There was power in Jesus' miracles, and there was power in His message as well. Jesus encouraged John not to give up hope.

56—JESUS TEACHES ABOUT JOHN THE BAPTIST (MATTHEW 11:7-19; LUKE 7:24-35).

After John the Baptist's disciples left, Jesus began to describe to the crowds the greatness of John's ministry. Some people present among that crowd had earlier made the journey to the Judean desert, listened to John's message, and been baptized. Jesus pointed out that John wasn't a celebrity, living in royal luxury. He was a prophet of God, the predicted forerunner of the predicted Messiah. Jesus said that John the Baptist was the greatest prophet who ever lived. But then Jesus assured His listeners that John's greatness would one day be eclipsed by the arrival of God's kingdom. Those who enter into the kingdom of God based on the death and resurrection of Jesus Christ enjoy even greater blessings than those who lived before Jesus' sacrificial death. The kingdom of God was advancing forcefully through the work of John the Baptist and Jesus Christ, but forceful men were opposing it. However, that kingdom would eventually overcome all opposition. Everyone who enters that kingdom through faith in Jesus Christ will experience a greatness of blessing and joy that far surpasses that of John the Baptist. Jesus then presented a picturesque illustration of those who resisted God's kingdom. Like children in a marketplace who make inconsistent and unachievable demands, those who resisted God's kingdom rejected both John the Baptist and Jesus. John lived an austere lifestyle, and his opponents accused him of being demon possessed. Jesus came with joy and celebration, and His opponents accused Him of frivolity. No one, not even Jesus, could please such a fickle crowd. Resistance was mounting, and Jesus addressed this opposition head on.

57—JESUS CONDEMNS THE UNBELIEVING CITIES (MATTHEW 11:20-30).

Jesus began to speak out boldly against those cities that had resisted His ministry during His preaching tours of Galilee. Specifically, Jesus identified Korazin and Bethsaida, two communities close to Capernaum. These cities had witnessed great miracles, yet had refused to repent. Jesus said that even the pagan Gentile cities of Tyre and Sidon would have repented under similar circumstances. Then Jesus accused His adopted home town of Capernaum of likewise resisting His ministry and message. Many people in and around Capernaum had benefited from Jesus' healing power, but apparently few had really followed Jesus with their hearts. Jesus declared that the ancient and wicked city of Sodom would have responded more favorably to Him than had Capernaum.

While Jesus condemned these unrepentant cities, He also offered a prayer of praise to His heavenly Father. Jesus thanked the Father for hiding the truth from the stubborn religious elite and for revealing it to innocent people who received it with childlike faith. In fact, Jesus Himself as God in the flesh played a determining role in revealing divine truth to those who would welcome it. As the heaven-sent revealer of truth, Jesus invited all who were weary and weighed down with life to come to Him for rest. "Take my yoke upon you," He said, "for my yoke is easy and my burden is light." Even in the midst of growing opposition to His ministry, Jesus offered help and hope to anyone who would follow Him.

#58—JESUS IS ANOINTED BY A SINFUL WOMAN AT A PHARISEE'S HOUSE (LUKE 7:36-50).

The Pharisees were often the most outspoken opponents of Jesus' ministry and message. One Pharisee invited Jesus to his home for dinner. During the course of the meal a woman who had a reputation for living a sinful life entered the Pharisee's home, weeping. She washed Jesus' feet with her tears and wiped them with her hair. She kissed His feet and poured perfume on them in an act of penitent faith. The Pharisee was appalled at this turn of events. He thought to himself that Jesus should have recognized this woman's sinful character if He were indeed a prophet of God.

Jesus knew what the Pharisee was thinking, and so asked the Pharisee a question. If a benefactor cancelled the debt of a man who owed him little and the debt of a man who owed him a great sum, which of the two debtors would be most grateful? The Pharisee rightly answered that the man who was forgiven the greater debt would have the greater love for his benefactor. Jesus then compared the Pharisee to the sinful woman. The Pharisee had not extended the usual courtesies of a host in that ancient culture, washing his guest's feet, greeting his guest with a kiss, or anointing his guest's head with oil. But the sinful woman had done all of these things in the most abject and grateful way she could. Unlike the pompous Pharisee, the sinful woman loved Jesus greatly. Jesus then turned to the sinful woman and declared to her that her sins were forgiven and that her faith had assured her of salvation. She could go in peace. The other guests who witnessed this event began to whisper among themselves, wondering how Jesus dared pronounce forgiveness of sins. Only God can forgive sins. Had they only realized that they were dining in the presence of God in the flesh they, too, could have received God's forgiveness and salvation.

Jesus' Fourth Galilean Tour and His Rejection at Nazareth

Jesus' third Galilean tour had ended on a note of rejection, both by certain unrepentant cities and by many of the religious leaders. Jesus would again resume His itinerant ministry, beginning His fourth Galilean tour. This tour would likewise see growing resistance to His ministry and it would again end in rejection.

159—JESUS' PREACHING AND FOLLOWING IN GALILEE (LUKE 8:1-3).

Luke's Gospel provides another summary of Jesus' ministry. Jesus traveled from town to town throughout Galilee proclaiming the good news of God's kingdom. His message had remained consistent during the course of

His public ministry. Luke also mentions that, in addition to Jesus' twelve disciples, a number of women followed Jesus closely in His ministry and provided resources for His work. Some of these women had been healed of sicknesses or released from demonic influences. Notable among these women was Mary Magdalene, a woman who had been demon possessed and now was a committed follower of Jesus her Savior.

60—JESUS' POWER IS ATTRIBUTED TO SATAN (MATTHEW 12:22-37; MARK 3:20-30).

While Jesus had many loyal followers, He also had a growing number of influential opponents. Those who opposed Jesus, however, had a problem on their hands. How could they discredit Jesus when He had performed so many amazing miracles? Even His own family members questioned Jesus' sanity in spite of His miracles. So, Jesus experienced resistance from a number of sources. On one occasion Jesus healed a demon possessed man who was both blind and mute. Those who witnessed this miracle began to refer to Jesus as the messianic Son of David. But the Pharisees and other religious leaders intervened. Enough was enough! Although they couldn't deny the reality of Jesus' miraculous power, they could attempt to discredit Him. Therefore, they told the crowd that Jesus performed His miracles by the power of Beelzebub, or Satan. Jesus, they claimed, was empowered by the devil, thus accounting for His power over demons. What a slap in the face to the holy Son of God!

Jesus immediately denied such a ridiculous accusation. After all, would Satan cast out Satan? Instead, Jesus was casting out demons by the power of God's Spirit, thereby proving that the kingdom of God was at hand. Jesus then warned that some who were present were in danger of committing an unforgivable sin by blaspheming the Holy Spirit. Although there is debate about the nature of this unpardonable sin, Jesus seems to have in mind a hardness of the human heart that refuses to acknowledge the true source of His supernatural work.

Jesus then, without mincing words, accused the Pharisees of displaying fruit that proved the wickedness in their hearts. He called them a brood of vipers, evil men who would one day give account before God for their slanderous words.

161—THE JEWISH LEADERS DEMAND A SIGN (MATTHEW 12:38-45).

The Pharisees and teachers of the law tried to turn the tables on Jesus' rebuke. They asked Jesus to perform a miracle that would once and for all signify to everyone that He was from God. Had they not witnessed more miracles than can be numbered? What would it take for these hardened hearts to accept Jesus?

Jesus saw through their duplicity. He refused to perform a special miracle for these skeptics, but did say that the one sign they should look for was that of the Old Testament prophet Jonah. Jonah had been in the belly of a huge fish for three days and three nights. Jesus said that He would be in the belly of the earth for three days and three nights. In other words, Jesus was pointing ahead to His death, burial, and resurrection. Jesus' resurrection would be the ultimate sign of His authority as the Son of God. After Jonah came out of the belly of the fish, he preached to the wicked people of Nineveh and they turned to God. One day the repentant people of Nineveh would stand in judgment against the people who were rejecting Jesus because Jesus was even greater than Jonah. Jesus was no minion of Satan. It was Jesus' opponents who were advancing Satan's causes. Jesus warned that their resistance would only bring greater harm to themselves and others. This encounter between Jesus and the resistant religious leaders proved to be a turning point in Jesus' ministry.

262—JESUS IDENTIFIES HIS TRUE MOTHER AND BROTHERS (MATTHEW 12:46-50; MARK 3:31-35; LUKE 8:19-21).

While Jesus was defending His ministry against the attacks of the Pharisees, His mother and brothers arrived outside the house where He was speaking. Someone sent word to Jesus that His family wanted to see Him. Jesus pointed to His disciples and said that those who obeyed the will of His heavenly Father were His true family. Jesus knew that His brothers didn't yet believe in Him. His family didn't understand Him. The religious leaders didn't want Him. But those who truly followed God also followed Jesus. These men and women of faith composed Jesus' true family, the family of God.

263—JESUS GIVES HIS PARABLE OF THE SOWER AND THE SOILS (MATTHEW 13:1-9; MARK 4:1-9; LUKE 8:4-8).

At this point in Jesus' ministry He began to make much greater use of parables in His public preaching.

Having been rejected by the national religious leaders, Jesus went out and sat beside the Sea of Galilee. Such a large crowd followed Jesus that He was forced to get into a boat from which He could teach the people. There, Jesus used a variety of parables to communicate concepts about the kingdom of God. For example, He told them a parable about a farmer sowing seed. The seed landed on four different kinds of soil. Some of the seed fell along the path where the birds came and ate it. Some fell on rocky soil and, though it sprouted, it couldn't take root and withered under the heat of the sun. Some fell among thorns which choked out its growth. But some of the seed fell on good soil and produced an abundant crop.

164—JESUS EXPLAINS HIS USE OF PARABLES (MATTHEW 13:10-17; MARK 4:10-12; LUKE 8:9-10).

What was Jesus saying through His parable of the soils, and why did He now use parables so extensively? Later that day the disciples asked Jesus these very questions. Jesus responded that He was both revealing and concealing truth by His use of parables. Those who were receptive to Jesus would gain greater understanding of spiritual truth through these parables. But through these same parables, spiritual truth would be hidden from those who rejected Jesus.

65—JESUS EXPLAINS HIS PARABLE OF THE SOWER AND THE SOILS (MATTHEW 13:18-23; MARK 4:13-20; LUKE 8:11-15).

Jesus then explained the parable of the soils to His disciples. The four soils represented varying conditions of the human heart. Some hearts are totally resistant to spiritual truth. The Word of God can't penetrate these hearts, and Satan snatches the truth away. Some hearts are receptive at first, but don't take God's Word seriously and the truth withers within them. Some hearts are too concerned about the things of the world around them, and these worldly cares choke out the truth. But some hearts are truly receptive to God's Word and produce lasting spiritual fruit.

66—JESUS GIVES HIS PARABLE OF THE WHEAT AND THE TARES (MATTHEW 13:24-30).

While Jesus was teaching the crowd that day He also presented His parable of the wheat and tares, or weeds. A farmer planted good seeds in his field, but at night an enemy planted tares in the farmer's field. When the seeds grew, it became apparent that there was a mixed crop. The farmer didn't want to uproot the tares for fear of destroying the good seed, so he let them grow together. He would separate the wheat from the tares at harvest time. Jesus would later explain this parable to His disciples as He had the parable of the soils.

1267—JESUS GIVES HIS PARABLE OF THE LAMP ON THE LAMP STAND (MARK 4:21-25; LUKE 8:16-18).

In His parable of the lamp and the lamp stand, Jesus described the kingdom of God as a lamp that gives light. We wouldn't put a lamp under a bowl or under a bed, but out in the open where its light can be seen. Likewise, the kingdom of God is to shine openly. We're not to hide what God is doing, but let our lights shine for Him.

1268—JESUS GIVES HIS PARABLE OF THE GROWING SEED (MARK 4:26-29).

Jesus again compared the kingdom of God to seeds. This time, however, Jesus described the mysterious and miraculous way in which seeds grow. The farmer has no control over the seed. The seed grows on its own, just as God designed it. God's kingdom will likewise grow supernaturally, apart from human effort.

1269—JESUS GIVES HIS PARABLE OF THE MUSTARD SEED (MATTHEW 13:31-32; MARK 4:30-34).

The parable of the mustard seed emphasizes the contrast between the tiny beginning of God's kingdom and its eventual expansive influence. The mustard seed was the smallest seed that farmers planted in ancient Israel. But from this tiny seed came a large plant, a tree that could even provide shelter for birds. God's kingdom began as a small movement of Jesus' followers, but has indeed spread around the world.

170—JESUS GIVES HIS PARABLE OF THE YEAST IN THE FLOUR (MATTHEW 13:33-35).

Jesus taught another parable about growth in God's kingdom. He said that yeast in a lump of dough spreads throughout the dough. Some see this parable as describing the ongoing growth of God's kingdom similar to the parable of the mustard seed. Others see the yeast as a symbol for sin and understand this parable as reflecting the ongoing presence of sin in the growing kingdom of God similar to the parable of the wheat and the tares. In either case, we know that God's kingdom will advance in spite of resistance. The religious leaders had been resisting Jesus' work, but His work would go on in spite of their opposition.

171—JESUS EXPLAINS HIS PARABLE OF THE WHEAT AND THE TARES (MATTHEW 13:36-43).

After Jesus had finished teaching the crowd, He went with His disciples into the house where they were staying. There, as we have already seen, Jesus explained the parable of the soils. Apparently He explained all of His parables to His disciples at that time. Matthew records Jesus' explanation of the parable of the wheat and the tares. A farmer sowed wheat in his field, but his enemy sowed tares. The field, Jesus said, is the world. The wheat represents believers and the tares represent unbelievers. The enemy is the devil. Both believers and unbelievers will continue to live side by side throughout the time of the expansion of God's kingdom. Eventually, however, unbelievers will be weeded out and cast into eternal judgment in hell. The righteous, however, will enjoy God's eternal, glorious reign.

972—JESUS GIVES HIS PARABLE OF THE HIDDEN TREASURE (MATTHEW 13:44).

Matthew's Gospel records three more parables that Jesus taught. The kingdom of God is like a treasure hidden in a field. When a man discovers that treasure, he sells everything he has and purchases the field along with its hidden treasure. This parable speaks of total commitment to Jesus and His kingdom.

973—JESUS GIVES HIS PARABLE OF THE PEARL OF GREAT PRICE (MATTHEW 13:45-46).

The kingdom of God, Jesus said, is also like a precious pearl. When a merchant finds such a valuable gem he sells everything he owns in order to purchase this pearl of great price. The kingdom of heaven is worthy of absolute personal sacrifice and commitment.

974—JESUS GIVES HIS PARABLE OF THE FISHING NET (MATTHEW 13:47-50).

Jesus also described the kingdom of God as a fishnet that draws in all kinds of fish, some edible and some of no value to the fisherman. The fisherman would separate the good fish from the bad, throwing the bad fish away. Likewise, the kingdom of God will for a time include both good and wicked people. But eventually God will send His angels to separate the good from the wicked, casting the wicked into eternal judgment. Thus, God's kingdom will be purified forever.

175—JESUS GIVES HIS PARABLE OF THE HOUSE OWNER'S TREASURES (MATTHEW 13:51-52).

Jesus completed His discourse on the kingdom of God by presenting one last parable. He asked His disciples if they understood everything He had taught, and they assured Jesus that they fully comprehended His teachings. Jesus didn't contest their assurance in their ability to grasp spiritual truths, but simply said that as teachers of God's law they would be like the owner of a house full of treasures. The owner of such a house might bring out old things or new for his guests to observe and enjoy. Likewise, anyone who is a teacher of God's truth can convey treasures from His Word that are both old and new, time tested yet fresh and alive.

Jesus' parables about the kingdom of God reflect His teaching that the kingdom would begin in a relatively small way, grow over time to a place of universal influence, and then be purged of evil so that righteousness will reign. That righteousness is possible only through Jesus' sacrificial death, a message worth sharing by all His followers.

5

THE MIDDLE GALILEAN MINISTRY OF JESUS (PART 2)

THE YEAR-LONG MIDDLE GALILEAN MINISTRY OF Jesus was characterized by increasing influence and increasing opposition. At the end of His third preaching tour of Galilee, Jesus reprimanded certain unrepentant cities for rejecting His message. During His fourth preaching tour the Pharisees overtly accused Jesus of operating out of Satan's power. Jesus then began to teach more frequently in parables in order to reveal truth to His followers but to conceal truth from His opponents. The Middle Galilean Ministry would conclude with the completion of Jesus' fourth preaching tour and a fifth preaching tour.

Jesus' Fourth Galilean Tour and His Rejection at Nazareth (Continued)

Jesus' fourth preaching tour continued to see growing opposition, culminating in His second biting rejection by His home town of Nazareth. Still, this preaching tour included many miraculous events. Countless lives experienced Jesus' powerful, compassionate, healing touch.

]976—JESUS CALMS THE STORM (MATTHEW 8:23-27; MARK 4:35-41; LUKE 8:22-25).

Mark's Gospel tells us that Jesus had had a very busy day. He had healed a demon possessed man, defended Himself against accusations of operating under Satan's power, and delivered His discourse on the kingdom of God. At the end of this busy day Jesus gave His disciples instructions to prepare a boat so that they could cross to the other side of the Sea of Galilee. For good reason, once Jesus was in the boat He fell fast asleep. However, as Jesus slept, a fierce storm suddenly blew over the Sea of Galilee. The waves rose and nearly swamped the boat. Even though several of Jesus' disciples were seasoned fishermen who were accustomed to conditions on the Sea of Galilee, even these men were afraid for their lives. They woke Jesus up, expressed their fear of drowning in these rough waves, and called on Jesus to save them. Jesus got up and rebuked the storm. Immediately the wind and the water grew calm. Jesus then assured His disciples that they need not fear, but should live by faith. These disciples had witnessed many miracles since they had been following Jesus, but this miracle of calming the storm produced a new level of amazement regarding their Master. They could hardly believe that even the winds and waves obeyed His voice.

77—JESUS HEALS TWO DEMON POSSESSED MEN AT GADARA (MATTHEW 8:28-34; MARK 5:1-20; LUKE 8:26-39).

After calming the storm on the Sea of Galilee, Jesus arrived with His disciples on the opposite shore in the Gentile territory of Gadara. Matthew's Gospel says that Jesus was met there by two demon possessed men, while Mark and Luke's Gospels refer only to one of these men, possibly the one being most significantly afflicted. These men lived among the tombs. They possessed such physical strength that even chains couldn't confine them. When these men saw Jesus, they, or rather the demons inside them, cried out in fear. They asked Jesus why He had come. Had He come to torment them before their appointed time of judgment? Jesus commanded the demons to leave these men. When the most outspoken demon begged for mercy, Jesus asked him to identify himself. The demon said that his name was Legion, and indicated that there were many demons within these two unfortunate victims. A Roman military legion consisted of 6,000 soldiers. Could there have been that many demons who had invaded the lives of these two men? Legion continued to beg Jesus for mercy, and asked to be transferred into a nearby herd of pigs rather than be sent off to eternal judgment. For reasons that only He knows, Jesus agreed to this request. Mark's Gospel tells us that there were about 2,000 pigs in the nearby herd. The demons left the bodies of the two men and entered into the herd of pigs. Immediately the pigs ran down the slope and drowned in the Sea of Galilee. The two men were freed, and the demons were gone forever.

News of this event quickly spread. Those who had been tending the herd of pigs ran into town to tell what had happened. The people of that town certainly knew about the former plight of the demon possessed men. They went out to see with their own eyes what was going on. They found the previously demon possessed men sitting at Jesus' feet having been restored to their normal senses. The people were so stunned and frightened by these events that they asked Jesus to leave their region. As Jesus was preparing to sail away, the men who had been demon possessed asked to go with Him. But Jesus instructed these men to go home to their families and testify to God's mercy and power. The men obeyed Jesus, and news about Jesus' power spread throughout the region.

78—JESUS HEALS AN UNCLEAN WOMAN AND RAISES JAIRUS' DAUGHTER FROM THE DEAD (MATTHEW 9:18-26; MARK 5:21-43; LUKE 8:40-56).

At their next landing point along the shore of the Sea of Galilee, Jesus and His disciples were met by another large crowd. One of the leaders of the local synagogue, a man by the name of Jairus, came to Jesus asking for help. He fell at Jesus' feet and begged Jesus to heal his dear, dying daughter. Jairus expressed his belief that if Jesus would go to his house and touch his daughter she would be healed. Jesus agreed to help.

However, as Jesus was making His way through the crowd, another miracle occurred. A certain woman in the crowd had been subject to bleeding for twelve years. Her condition would have rendered her ceremonially unclean according to Jewish law, excluding her from religious functions and social contacts. This unclean woman believed that if she could simply touch Jesus' garment she would be healed. As the crowd followed Jesus, the woman reached out and touched the edge of His cloak. Immediately she was healed of her bleeding.

Jesus knew that healing power had flowed from Him, and turned to see who had touched Him. His disciples suggested that the touch was simply the brush of the crowd, but Jesus knew differently. At last the woman stepped forward, fell at Jesus' feet, and fearfully revealed her story. Jesus reassured the woman that her faith had healed her, and told her she could go in peace.

This miraculous act of healing was a source of great joy to the woman who had touched Jesus' garment. However, it also caused a delay in Jesus' arrival at Jairus' house where this man's daughter lay dying. Jairus must have been impatient with anxiety. Then, his worst fears were realized. While Jesus had taken time to heal the unclean woman, He had missed His opportunity to help Jairus' daughter. News came that the girl had died. The servants who delivered this sad news told Jairus that he need bother Jesus no more. It was too late.

Jesus reassured Jairus, telling him not to be afraid but to have faith. When they arrived at Jairus' house, Jesus was met by a gathering of people who were loudly mourning the girl's death. Jesus told them that the girl wasn't dead but merely sleeping. To Jesus, death is but sleep. After all, Jesus has the power of life. The mourners ridiculed Jesus' statement and Jesus sent them out of the house. He took Peter, James, and John along with the girl's mother and father into the dead girl's bedroom. Then Jesus took the girl by the hand and said, "Little girl, I tell you to get up." The girl, who was twelve years old, immediately stood to her feet and walked around. She was again alive and well. The girl's parents were amazed. Jesus instructed them not to tell what had happened, but news spread quickly about this event. Jesus was able to heal the sick, and He was even able to raise the dead!

79—JESUS HEALS TWO BLIND MEN (MATTHEW 9:27-31).

As Jesus walked along, two blind men pursued Him and asked Him to show them mercy. Jesus went inside a house where there would be more privacy. He asked the blind men if they believed He could restore their sight. The two blind men affirmed their faith in Jesus' healing power. Jesus touched their eyes and assured them that their faith had been rewarded. Immediately the two men could see. Jesus instructed these two men not to tell what had happened, but they couldn't contain their enthusiasm. They told people all around the region what Jesus had done for them. Jesus' reluctance to have news about Him spread seems to have been motivated by the fact that He knew many were following Him simply to benefit from His miraculous power rather than to respond to His message of repentance. But more and more people became aware of Jesus' ability to heal the sick.

80—JESUS DELIVERS A DEMON POSSESSED MAN WHO WAS MUTE (MATTHEW 9:32-34).

While the two men whom Jesus had healed of blindness were leaving the house, another man was brought to Jesus for help. This man was demon possessed. Apparently, demon possession can manifest itself through any number of physical symptoms. Some who were demon possessed demonstrated violent behavior, while others were blind, and still others had various illnesses. Not every physical illness was a result of demonic influence, but some illnesses indeed had demons as their root cause. Jesus knew the difference and helped each individual according to his or her need. The demon possessed man who was brought to Jesus for help that day was mute, unable to speak. Jesus drove the demon out of the man and the man began to speak. The crowd was again amazed at Jesus' power. However, the Pharisees continued to attribute Jesus' power to Satan.

81—JESUS' FINAL REJECTION AT NAZARETH (MATTHEW 13:53-58; MARK 6:1-6).

It wasn't just the Pharisees and other religious leaders who rejected Jesus. Those who knew Jesus best, those from Nazareth who had seen Him grow up, were numbered among Jesus' skeptics. Jesus had already been rejected at Nazareth earlier in His ministry. At that time the people attempted to cast Him off a cliff, but Jesus walked away unharmed. Jesus returned to Nazareth at the end of His fourth preaching tour of Galilee. It seems that Jesus wanted to give His home town a second chance to acknowledge Him as the Son of God. He again went to the synagogue and began to teach. The people who heard Him were amazed at His wisdom and His reputation for miraculous power. After all, they knew Him as a carpenter. They knew His mother Mary. They knew His brothers and sisters. They seemed to know everything about Jesus except the fact that He was their promised Messiah, the Son of God. Once again, though less violently, the people of Nazareth expressed their disbelief in Jesus. Jesus told them that a prophet is without honor only in his home town. Because the people of Nazareth didn't believe in Jesus, He was unable to perform many miracles there. Mark's Gospel tells us that Jesus did heal a few sick people in Nazareth. However, much to Jesus' amazement and probably His sorrow, those who knew Jesus best refused to believe in Him.

Jesus' Fifth Galilean Tour and His Rejection by the Uncommitted

Jesus' third preaching tour had ended in rejection by several unrepentant cities. His fourth tour witnessed His official rejection by the religious leaders who attributed His power to Satan and ended with His rejection at Nazareth. Jesus now embarked on His fifth

Galilean tour. This preaching tour would, likewise, end in rejection. However, during this fifth Galilean tour Jesus would send out His twelve apostles to broaden His work and touch many more lives with the message of God's kingdom.

182—JESUS TEACHES THROUGHOUT GALILEE (MATTHEW 9:35-38).

As with His other preaching tours, Jesus went throughout the towns and villages of Galilee. In each location Jesus would teach in the synagogues, proclaiming the good news of God's kingdom. He would also heal the sick and show them God's love. Jesus recognized the plight of the common people of Galilee. They were hurting and helpless, like sheep without a shepherd who could nurture and protect them. Jesus loved these needy people. He also knew that others would have to share His love for the people and join Him in meeting their needs. He told His disciples that the harvest was great, but the workers were few. He then challenged His disciples to pray that the Lord God might send more workers into this needy harvest field. There are still many spiritually needy people today, and we must pray for God to send us and others among them in order to reach them with the good news of Jesus Christ.

183—JESUS SENDS OUT THE TWELVE APOSTLES (MATTHEW 10:1-42; MARK 6:7-13; LUKE 9:1-6).

At this point in His ministry, Jesus engaged a new strategy for meeting the vast needs of the people. For many months Jesus had been training His disciples by word and example. Now the time had come for them to go out on their own and advance God's work. In order for these twelve apostles to accomplish this work, Jesus granted them authority to drive out demons, to heal all kinds of illnesses, and even to raise the dead. Along with these miraculous powers, the twelve disciples received Jesus' authorization to proclaim the good news of God's kingdom.

As Jesus was sending out His twelve apostles, He gave them specific instructions about their impending ministry. They were to work exclusively among the Jewish people, avoiding for the present time the Gentile and Samaritan population centers. They were to be generous in the use of their power. "Feely you have received," Jesus told them, "so freely give." The disciples were to take no provisions for themselves—no money or extra clothing. Instead, they were to depend on God and God's people to meet their needs. As they entered a town, they were to identify a worthy host and remain in that home during their stay in that community rather than trying to better their situation. If these representatives of Jesus experienced rejection, they were to shake the dust from their feet and leave that town. Jesus knew that they would in fact face opposition. He described His disciples as sheep among wolves. Therefore, Jesus warned them to be as wise as serpents, yet as harmless as doves.

This particular period of ministry would prepare these disciples for future outreach that would include even more intense persecution. One day these men would be arrested, flogged, and taken before the Gentile authorities for even more severe punishment. Jesus warned in advance that in those days His followers could depend on the Holy Spirit to give them the words they would need to say. Persecution for Jesus would include rejection by family members and hatred by the masses. However, God would preserve His messengers.

But why would those who spread the loving, life-giving message of the gospel experience such hatred and rejection? Jesus said that a servant is not above his master. Since Jesus had been rejected, even to the point of being accused of working by means of Satan's power, His followers would experience similar persecution. But Jesus assured His followers that they need not fear persecution. Those who persecute can at most kill the body, not the soul. Furthermore, God knows the minutest detail of our lives. He cares for us supremely. Therefore, no one should be ashamed of following Jesus. Jesus' ministry on earth didn't produce peace, but separation and hardship. Anyone who wants to truly follow Jesus must accept such difficulties as the cost of discipleship. That cost, however, carries with it unspeakable reward.

Having commissioned His twelve disciples, Jesus sent them on their way. They went from village to village preaching the good news of God's kingdom, challenging people to repent. As they went they cast out demons and, anointing the sick with oil, healed many people in many different places.

384—JESUS TRAVELS THROUGHOUT GALILEE ALONE (MATTHEW 11:1).

Having sent out His twelve disciples, Jesus Himself went out teaching and preaching from town to town. Matthew's Gospel seems to imply that Jesus carried on this brief ministry tour throughout Galilee alone. Jesus was now working through His disciples, but He continued to work directly among the needy people of Galilee.

385—HEROD EXECUTES JOHN THE BAPTIST (MATTHEW 14:1-12; MARK 6:14-29; LUKE 9:7-9).

One man who took special interest in Jesus, albeit for sinister reasons, was King Herod Antipas. Herod had previously arrested John the Baptist for preaching against his hedonistic lifestyle. Herod had been so blatantly disobedient to God's law that he had gone so far as to marry his own brother's wife, Herodias. Later, Herod threw a birthday banquet in his own honor. As he drank with his guests, Herodias' daughter danced for those in attendance. Her dance so impressed Herod that he promised her any gift she might ask up to half his kingdom. Being coached by the hatred of her mother, the girl asked Herod for the head of John the Baptist. Now, it was one thing to imprison a prophet of God. It was still another to put a prophet of God to death. Nevertheless, Herod felt the pressure of his guests to comply with the girl's simple, though ghastly, request. He sent an executioner who soon returned with John's head on a platter. John's disciples secured the body of this outstanding prophet of God and provided a proper burial. Then they went and told Jesus. We can only imagine the grief that must have pierced Jesus' heart at such tragic news.

Reports of Jesus' growing influence in Galilee troubled Herod greatly. Some people were saying that John the Baptist had risen from the dead. Others said that Jesus was the ancient prophet Elijah who had returned to earth. Still others simply declared Jesus to be a great prophet like some of the other prophets of old. Herod anticipated that, even if Jesus wasn't John the Baptist alive from the dead, this new prophet would cause him as much trouble as John. Herod, Luke's Gospel tells us, tried to see Jesus, but was apparently unsuccessful. He would, however, continue to hear about this man who claimed to be God and who demonstrated the miraculous power of God.

186—THE RETURN OF THE TWELVE APOSTLES (MARK 6:30-31).

The twelve apostles eventually returned to Jesus after completing their itinerant ministry throughout the towns of Galilee. They were eager to report about their work, and Jesus must have been pleased with their progress. He also knew their limitations. Because people were constantly surrounding Him and His disciples, Jesus told His disciples to follow Him to a secluded place for rest. Jesus may have needed time away from the crowds in order to reflect on the death of John the Baptist. The disciples needed rest from their intensive time of ministry. Reflection, rest, and prayer are essential elements for serving God.

87—JESUS FEEDS THE FIVE THOUSAND (MATTHEW 14:13-21; MARK 6:32-44; LUKE 9:10-17; JOHN 6:1-14).

Jesus and His disciples got into a boat and sailed away to seek a secluded place of rest. But it seemed impossible for Jesus to escape the attention of the crowd. As soon as Jesus and His disciples brought the boat to shore, people from all over had gathered to see Him. Though exhausted, Jesus recognized the needs of these helpless sheep. He had compassion for them and began once again to teach and heal the growing multitude.

As the day wore on, the people grew hungry. Many had left their homes abruptly at the news of Jesus' arrival and hadn't brought along any kind of provisions. The disciples pointed out this need to Jesus. They encouraged Jesus to dismiss the crowd, sending them into the neighboring villages to find food. But Jesus caught His disciples off guard by telling them to feed the people. The disciples couldn't imagine how they might secure enough food for everyone to get even a taste. They quickly calculated that it would take eight months' wages to pay for such a feast. Jesus asked His disciples to take inventory. What did they have? Andrew found a boy who had packed a small lunch. All that was available to feed this great crowd were five small loaves of bread and two small fish. The disciples had only this minuscule meal, but they also had Jesus!

Jesus instructed the disciples to organize the crowd, seating them in groups along the grassy hillside. He then looked up to heaven, thanked His heavenly Father for the five loaves and two fish, and began to break the bread and fish for distribution by His disciples. It's not hard to imagine the joy in Jesus' eyes and the amazement in the eyes of His disciples as the bread and fish kept coming. Everyone in that massive crowd ate all they wanted. At the end of the feast, the disciples counted twelve baskets full of leftovers. They also calculated that there were five thousand men present, not counting women and children. One of those uncounted children, a small boy, had provided a great service by offering his lunch to Jesus. This miracle stood out so much in the minds of Jesus' disciples that, apart from Jesus' resurrection, the feeding of the five thousand is the only miracle recorded in all four Gospels.

#88—JESUS WALKS ON THE WATER (MATTHEW 14:22-33; MARK 6:45-52; JOHN 6:15-21).

After Jesus miraculously fed the five thousand, some who were present became more and more convinced that Jesus was the promised prophet and Messiah. They began to talk about making Jesus their king, using force if necessary. Jesus knew their intentions, and He also knew that His path to the throne had to go by way of a cross. Therefore, He instructed His disciples to take a boat to the opposite shore of the Sea of Galilee while He stayed behind to dismiss the crowd. After the crowd dissipated, Jesus spent several hours in private prayer. From His vantage point on shore, Jesus could see His disciples' boat. A wind had risen on the Sea of Galilee, and the disciples were laboring hard at the oars to overcome the force of the wind and waves.

Sometime in the early hours before sunrise, Jesus performed yet another extraordinary miracle. He walked across the water to meet His disciples in their boat. As He caught up with their boat, they made out His figure and were terrified. They thought they were seeing a ghost. Jesus reassured them by calling out and identifying Himself to His disciples.

Peter responded to Jesus by asking Jesus to invite him out on the water. Jesus said to Peter, "Come." Peter stepped out of the boat onto the stormy waves and began to walk toward Jesus. But then Peter took note of the storm around him and started to sink into the water. Jesus reached out His hand, lifted Peter to safety, and gently rebuked this audacious disciple for his lack of faith. Once Jesus and Peter climbed into the boat the wind died down.

The disciples were amazed and worshiped Jesus, calling Him the Son of God. Mark's Gospel points out that even after all they'd witnessed, including the feeding of the five thousand, the disciples had trouble fully understanding Jesus' true power and identity. They still had hard hearts. Spiritual truths sink in slowly for most people. These disciples were growing, be it ever so slowly, in their faith in Jesus.

89—JESUS HEALS THE MULTITUDES AT GENNESARET (MATTHEW 14:34-36; MARK 6:53-56).

The morning after Jesus fed the five thousand and walked to His disciples on the water He arrived in the region of Gennesaret. Gennesaret rested along the western shore of the Sea of Galilee near Capernaum. When He and His disciples got out of the boat, the people recognized Him immediately and sent word throughout the region that Jesus had arrived. Soon, people were bringing their sick friends and relatives to Jesus, believing that by simply touching the edge of His cloak they would be healed. In fact, everyone who touched Jesus did experience His healing power. All throughout the towns and villages Jesus healed the sick and taught the message of God's kingdom.

90—JESUS PRESENTS HIS BREAD OF LIFE DISCOURSE (JOHN 6:22-71).

As His fifth preaching tour of Galilee drew to a close, Jesus challenged the people who were following Him to deepen their commitment. The day after Jesus fed the five thousand, the crowd searched for Him and eventually found Him and His disciples at Capernaum. Although it should have been gratifying to know that the people wanted to be near Him, Jesus knew that deep down the crowd was following Him for the wrong reasons. Many of the people were enamored with His miracles, but had thus far rejected His message. It was at this stage in Jesus' ministry that He presented His Bread of Life Discourse. In this extended conversation with those who had gathered in the synagogue at Capernaum, Jesus explained that following Him demanded an all-out commitment.

Jesus began this discourse by rightly accusing the crowd of pursuing Him simply because He'd fed them physical food. Instead, they should have been hungry for spiritual food, food that would result in eternal life. The people asked what they had to do to receive such spiritual food. What work did God require of them? Jesus simply stated that they need only believe in Him, the One whom God the Father had sent into the world. Faith, true faith in Jesus Christ, is God's only requirement for entering into eternal life.

At this point the people betrayed their shallow hearts. They asked Jesus to perform a miraculous sign to verify His message, claiming that they would then believe in Him. They pointed to Moses as an example of a great prophet. Moses, they said, had fed their forefathers manna during an extended period of time in the wilderness. Shouldn't Jesus likewise continually give them bread to eat? The crowd, having been miraculously fed only the day before, wanted to be fed again. They demanded more miracles, more food, but they refused to put their faith in Jesus.

Jesus responded to the crowd's unreasonable demand by pointing out that it wasn't Moses who fed the people in the wilderness, but God. Furthermore, it is God the Father who offers true bread from heaven. Jesus declared Himself to be that bread. He is the one who came down from His Father in heaven. He is the only one who can give life to this spiritually lifeless world.

The crowd then asked Jesus to give them the kind of bread He was describing, the kind of bread that would assure them of eternal life. They didn't yet recognize that the bread of life was standing right in front of them. So Jesus stated plainly, "I am the bread of life." He then explained that anyone who would come to Him by faith would never hunger or thirst again. Jesus then warned the people that even though they had seen Him and witnessed His miraculous work, they still refused to believe in Him. They were still resistant to God the Father. God, however, would give many people to Jesus, and Jesus would accept any and all whom the Father would send to Him. In fact, Jesus declared that it is the Father's will that everyone who looks to Jesus through the eyes of faith will have eternal life and be raised to live forever at the final judgment of God.

The people now became irritated with Jesus' claim to be the bread of life. They grumbled, saying that this Jesus was merely the son of a local carpenter. Many of the people knew Jesus' family personally, and yet Jesus was claiming that God was uniquely His Father. Jesus knew their hearts, and told them to stop grumbling. He stated that no one can come to faith in Him unless the Father draws that person. They would need to listen to God. They would need to accept God's message that Jesus is the bread of life. As the bread of life, Jesus would give His life for the world.

Again the crowd took offense at Jesus' words. They thought Jesus was saying that they would have to eat His flesh just like they might eat a loaf of bread. Jesus replied that they would indeed have to eat His flesh and drink His blood. He was not, of course, speaking in literal terms but in the sense that faith is an inward response that permeates every part of our lives. Everyone who thus consumes Jesus by faith has eternal life. Faith produces a lasting, intimate relationship.

At this point many of Jesus' more remote followers, whom John's Gospel refers to as disciples in the broad sense of this term, decided that Jesus was demanding too much from them. Jesus challenged them by saying that if His teaching about being the bread of life offended them, they would never be able to handle His future ascent to heaven. Jesus came from heaven and would return to heaven. To deny His heavenly origin would make it impossible to accept the fact that His departure meant returning to His eternal home. Jesus acknowledged that many who heard Him that day refused to believe. In fact, because He is God in the flesh, Jesus knew from the beginning who didn't believe in Him and who would eventually betray Him. At the end of Jesus' Bread of Life Discourse, many of His followers abandoned Him. This call to commitment was too intense for their loyalty. They enjoyed being with Jesus when He fed them physical food, but they wanted nothing to do with Him as their spiritual Lord.

Jesus then turned to His twelve most loyal disciples, the twelve apostles. He asked if they, too, wanted to leave Him. Peter, speaking on behalf of the twelve, declared his unflinching loyalty to Jesus. After all, only Jesus spoke the truth about eternal life. Only Jesus was "the Holy One of God." Jesus then said that He had indeed hand selected these twelve disciples. Yet sadly, among the twelve was hiding an adversary, a devil. Because Jesus knows the human heart, He already knew that Judas would eventually betray Him.

Jesus concluded His fifth preaching tour and His Middle Galilean Ministry on a note of widespread rejection. Yet Jesus still had followers, true followers who believed in His message and were growing in their faith. His message is still true today. Jesus is the bread of life. When we bring Jesus into our lives by faith He grants us satisfying, everlasting life.

6

THE LATER GALILEAN
MINISTRY OF JESUS

JESUS' EARLY GALILEAN MINISTRY SAW GROWING support for His message and His miracles. His Middle Galilean Ministry brought about growing opposition, particularly when Jesus began to crystallize His call to commitment among so many who had been following Him purely for the sake of His miracles. During His Later Galilean Ministry, Jesus began to speak more openly about His impending death and ultimate resurrection. This later ministry in Galilee included two final preaching tours, both of which stretched beyond the confines of the Jewish population centers. Jesus sought solitude from the crowds in order to instruct His disciples, traveling as far as Tyre and Caesarea-Philippi.

Jesus' Sixth Galilean Tour and His Journey to Tyre

According to John 6:4, the Jewish feast of Passover was near when Jesus fed the five thousand. He gave His Bread of Life Discourse the next day. While John's Gospel doesn't state that Jesus went to Jerusalem for that Passover, it had been Jesus' pattern to attend the Passover celebration in Jerusalem. The Bread of Life Discourse and its subsequent Passover, therefore, become an appropriate place to distinguish between Jesus' Middle and Later Galilean Ministries. After the time of the Passover, Jesus traveled north through Galilee to the Gentile cities of Tyre and Sidon. These cities were in the ancient region of Phoenicia, which had become a part of the larger Roman province of Syria. Eventually, Jesus would wind His way southeast of the Sea of Galilee through the Gentile city district known as the Decapolis, or the Ten Cities. Jesus was obviously avoiding further work among the Jewish population that had previously rejected His message. But Jesus would eventually end this sixth preaching tour near His adopted home town of Capernaum.

<u>#91—JESUS DEFENDS HIS DISCIPLES (MATTHEW 15:1-20; MARK 7:1-23).</u>

Some of the Pharisees had followed Jesus from Jerusalem back to Galilee. They immediately found another excuse to accuse Jesus of moral impropriety. This time they focused their accusations on ceremonial washing. The Pharisees often washed their hands as a part of their public rituals in order to remind themselves and others about God's purity. However, Jesus never instructed His disciples to perform such rituals. He was more concerned about inner purity, purity of the heart. When the Pharisees observed that Jesus' disciples didn't engage in such rituals they asked Jesus why He allowed His followers to violate these customs.

Jesus lashed back at their pretentious accusations. He called the Pharisees hypocrites. Quoting the prophet Isaiah, Jesus warned that the Pharisees honored God with their lips but not with their hearts. They followed human rules but failed to worship God in any meaningful way. Jesus gave an example of their hypocrisy. He reminded the Pharisees that the law teaches us to honor our parents. However, the Pharisees had devised a system whereby a person could claim that his or her wealth was devoted to God and therefore could not be used to assist an aging father or mother. This was clearly a violation of God's law.

Apparently a crowd began to gather as Jesus spoke these appropriately harsh words to the Pharisees. Addressing this growing crowd, Jesus said that it isn't what's on the outside that counts, but what's on the inside. What we put into our mouths doesn't make us unclean in God's sight. What makes us unclean is what comes out of our mouths, our words and attitudes that reveal our sinful hearts. It is the heart that God judges.

The disciples then told Jesus that the Pharisees had taken offense at His words. Jesus instructed His disciples not to be enamored with the Pharisees. The Pharisees were blind guides leading spiritually blind men and women farther away from God. God would eventually pluck up these blind leaders and discard them like weeds.

Later, when the disciples were alone with Jesus, Peter asked Him to explain the parable about unclean food and unclean hearts. Jesus expressed His disappointment that the disciples hadn't already caught on to His message. He explained that anything we eat simply passes through our bodies. But what comes out of our mouths reveals our hearts. Our hearts are filled with evil thoughts, murder, adultery, and lies. These are the things that make us unclean in God's sight. These are the things for which Jesus came to die on the cross. Incidentally, Mark's Gospel comments that Jesus' lesson on unclean foods also was His way of declaring all foods clean, in contrast to the kosher regulations of the Old Testament.

#92—JESUS DELIVERS THE DAUGHTER OF A SYRO-PHOENICIAN WOMAN (MATTHEW 15:21-28; MARK 7:24-30).

Jesus now led His disciples north to the region of Tyre and Sidon. The distance involved must have provided Jesus extended time to teach the disciples, preparing them for what was ahead. But even in that region news had spread about Jesus. A Gentile woman—Matthew's Gospel calls her a Canaanite, while Mark's refers to her as a Greek woman from Syrian Phoenicia—came to Jesus for help. Though a Gentile, this woman called Jesus the Son of David and told Him that her daughter was demon possessed. At first Jesus didn't respond.

The woman apparently persisted in her request for help to the point that the disciples asked Jesus to send her away. Jesus said that He had been sent to help only the lost sheep of Israel. The woman, however, knelt before Jesus and begged for His help. Jesus told the woman that it wasn't right to take the children's bread and give it to the dogs, implying that the Jews and not the Gentiles were to be the recipients of God's blessings. This may seem like a cruel statement from the lips of Jesus. But we can also imagine that Jesus communicated through His eyes and expressions an invitation for this woman to press Him on the matter. Was He not teaching His disciples that eventually even the Gentiles would be the recipients of the gospel that was first offered to and often rejected by the Jews?

The woman did indeed persist in her request. She said to Jesus that even dogs benefit from the crumbs that fall from the table. Couldn't she benefit from one of Jesus' miracles? Jesus acknowledged the Syro-Phoenician woman's faith and granted her request. When the woman arrived home, she found her daughter completely freed from her demon possession.

193—JESUS HEALS A DEAF MAN (MATTHEW 15:29-31; MARK 7:31-37).

Having spent an undisclosed amount of time in the region of Tyre and Sidon, Jesus then led His disciples back to the Sea of Galilee and on to the Gentile region of the Decapolis southeast of the lake. There, some people brought a man to Jesus and begged for Jesus to heal him. The man was deaf and barely capable of speech. Jesus took the man aside from the crowd, put His fingers in the man's ears, spit and touched the man's tongue, looked up to heaven, and said, "Be opened." Instantly the man's ears were opened so that he could hear and his tongue loosened so that he could speak. Why Jesus used this method to heal this particular man is known only to Him. We might assume, however, that Jesus used the appropriate method of healing in each particular case to bolster the faith of the one being healed. Sometimes Jesus simply spoke a word, while sometimes He touched a person. Jesus works with each of us in the way He deems best.

After healing the deaf man, Jesus was again surrounded by crowds of needy people. He freely healed all who came. The people of the Decapolis were amazed that Jesus could make mute tongues speak, lame legs walk, and blind eyes see. Though many of these people whom Jesus healed were probably Gentiles, they praised the God of Israel because of Jesus' miraculous work.

94—JESUS FEEDS THE FOUR THOUSAND (MATTHEW 15:32-39; MARK 8:1-10).

The crowd that had gathered around Jesus was so committed to Him that they stayed with Him for three full days. They had no food, but they had something better. They had Jesus! Jesus felt great compassion for this crowd of committed men and women. He knew that if He sent them away, their physical strength might wear out before they arrived home. So Jesus told His disciples to provide food for the crowd. The disciples asked Jesus where they could find food for so many in such a remote place. Did these disciples suspect that Jesus might again miraculously feed a multitude? Jesus asked how much food they had. The disciples had only seven loaves of bread and a few small fish.

Once again Jesus instructed His disciples to have

the crowd sit down. Once again Jesus gave thanks to God the Father for the limited supply of food. Once again Jesus began to break apart the bread and the fish. Once again the entire crowd ate all they wanted. Once again the disciples gathered the leftovers, this time seven baskets full of bread and fish. Once again Jesus must have smiled as He saw the crowd fed and the disciples amazed. That day about four thousand men, plus women and children, benefited from Jesus' miraculous provision. After Jesus fed the four thousand, He sent the crowd away. He then got into a boat with His disciples and went to the northern shore of the Sea of Galilee near a town called Magadan. Mark's Gospel calls the region Dalmanutha.

95—THE PHARISEES REQUEST A SIGN (MATTHEW 16:1-4; MARK 8:11-13).

Having returned to primarily Jewish territory, Jesus was again accosted by the Pharisees and another Jewish sect called the Sadducees. They questioned Him and once again asked Him to show them a miraculous sign to verify His authority. Jesus had little time for such nonsense. He simply accused these religious leaders of being better able to read weather patterns than to read the signs of God's work. He warned His questioners that only a wicked generation would require a sign. Jesus once again told them that the only sign they would receive was that of the prophet Jonah. Earlier, Jesus had stated that, just as Jonah had been in the belly of the fish for three days and nights, He would be in the belly of the earth for three days and nights. Jesus said that His death and resurrection would be the only sign He would give. That sign should have been sufficient for Jesus' most adamant opponents. Even today, Jesus' death and resurrection should be all we need to trust and follow Him. Having answered His critics along the shore of the Sea of Galilee near Magadan, Jesus got back into the boat and sailed to another coastal town, the fishing village of Bethsaida.

96—JESUS WARNS ABOUT THE YEAST OF THE PHARISEES (MATTHEW 16:5-12; MARK 8:14-21).

As Jesus and His disciples were sailing toward Bethsaida, Jesus warned the disciples to beware of the yeast of the Pharisees, the Sadducees, and even Herod. The disciples were puzzled about this statement. What did Jesus mean? Was He talking about bread? After all, the disciples had neglected to bring any food along with them in the boat.

Jesus became aware of His disciples' confusion, and again reprimanded them for their lack of faith. Why were their hearts so hardened that they could not see the truth? After all, Jesus pointed out, they had previously witnessed the feeding of the five thousand and then, just the day before, had witnessed the feeding of the four thousand. Would Jesus really be concerned about a lack of bread? Of course not! Jesus was warning His disciples to be on guard against the teachings of the Pharisees and Sadducees. Their false teachings had spread like yeast in a batch of dough. But the legalism of the Pharisees and the syncretism of the Sadducees could never lead a person to God. We need to discern truth from error. We need to constantly be on the lookout for false teachings, being careful to declare and defend the truth of Jesus Christ as recorded in His Word.

Jesus' Seventh Galilean Tour and His Journey to Caesarea-Philippi

Jesus and His disciples had traveled throughout the Gentile territory of Syria and the Decapolis during His sixth Galilean tour. During His seventh and final preaching tour in the region of Galilee, Jesus began intentionally directing His disciples' attention toward the future. Jesus would soon die a horrible death, but He would also rise again. His disciples needed to have a clear understanding of His identity as the messianic Son of God in order to weather the difficult road ahead.

197—JESUS HEALS A BLIND MAN (MARK 8:22-26).

Jesus and His disciples arrived at Bethsaida, a small fishing community on the shore of the Sea of Galilee near Capernaum. There, some people brought a blind man to Jesus. They asked Jesus to apply His healing touch to their friend. Jesus led the blind man outside the village, spit on the man's eyes, then tenderly placed His hands on the man's eyes. He then asked the man what he could see. The man replied that he could see only indistinctly. To him, men looked like trees walking around. Jesus again put His hands on the man's eyes, at which point the man could see perfectly. Then Jesus sent the man home, telling him not to return to the village, apparently so that no greater notoriety would surround Jesus. The healing of this blind man was the only recorded miracle that Jesus performed in stages. Is it possible that the blind man's faith needed to grow in stages, and Jesus, who knows our hearts, accommodated this man's growing faith? Jesus meets us where we are and leads us into a closer walk with Him.

98—Peter Confesses Jesus as the Messiah (Matthew 16:13-20; Mark 8:27-30; Luke 9:18-21).

From Bethsaida, Jesus led His disciples north to the city of Caesarea-Philippi in the foothills of Mount Hermon. In that remote region Jesus pressed His disciples with a question that still challenges hearts today. He asked them, "Who do people say I am?" An accurate identification of Jesus is essential to our faith. The disciples told Jesus that some people thought He was John the Baptist. Others thought Jesus was one of the prophets, either Elijah, Jeremiah, or one of the other prophets of old who had come back to life. Apparently it had been difficult for many people, in spite of His many miracles, to acknowledge Jesus in His own right as the Son of God, the promised Messiah.

Jesus then posed the question directly to His disciples, asking, "What about you? Who do you say that I am?" While others may misunderstand or underestimate Jesus, we must see Him for who He really is. As often seems to have been the case, Peter spoke on behalf of the rest of the disciples. There in the shadow of Mount Hermon, Peter said, "You are the Christ, the Son of the living God."

The disciples correctly identified Jesus as their Messiah, God's unique Son.

Jesus affirmed Peter's statement. He told Peter that the truth of his confession was not revealed to him by human means, but God the Father had made Jesus' identity known to these disciples. Jesus went on to further affirm Peter's character and role. He referred to Peter's name, which means "rock," and stated that He would build His church upon this rock. Even the gates of hell wouldn't prevail against the church. This was Jesus' first reference to the church. Jesus was beginning to point His disciples to the future, including His death, His resurrection, and His new community of believers known as the church.

There has been a great deal of debate about Jesus' statement. Who or what was the "rock" upon which Jesus would build His church? Was it Peter as the leader of the apostles, or was it the truth of Peter's statement identifying Jesus as the Messiah? Whichever interpretation we might choose, the main point of Jesus' statement is that He would build His church. The church is Christ's ordained institution, His body on earth. He promised to build, bless, and protect His church.

Jesus also promised to give to Peter the keys to the kingdom of heaven, saying that whatever Peter might bind on earth would be bound in heaven and whatever he might free on earth would be freed in heaven. This statement, likewise, has generated much debate. Did Peter receive some special authority over people's destinies? It seems preferable to conclude that Jesus was simply granting the apostles the special opportunity of opening various doors of ministry.

Jesus affirmed Peter's identification of Him as the Messiah, but He also instructed His disciples not to tell anyone about His identity. He had clearly presented Himself as the Messiah, but people would have to come to this conclusion on their own as a faith response to His message. We, too, must correctly identify who Jesus is. Through the eyes of faith we must acknowledge Jesus as our Messiah, our Savior, and our God.

99—Jesus Teaches about His Death (Matthew 16:21-23; Mark 8:31-33; Luke 9:22).

Peter's confession of Jesus as the Christ served as a turning point in Jesus' ministry. Now, Jesus began to speak openly to His disciples about His impending death and resurrection. Jesus came to die for our sins. He had to fulfill His mission. Jesus told His disciples that He must go to Jerusalem where He would be rejected by the Jewish leaders and put to death. After three days He would rise from the dead. These straightforward statements by Jesus prompted Peter to pull Jesus aside and rebuke Him. Peter said that he would never let Jesus go through such an ignominious ordeal. But Jesus rebuked Peter for his failure to grasp the whole plan of redemption. Jesus looked through Peter to the true enemy of God's redemptive plan, Satan. He said to Peter, "Get behind me Satan." Peter's desire to prevent Jesus from going to the cross was actually contrary to God's plan. Without Jesus' death we cannot enter into eternal life.

#100—JESUS TEACHES ABOUT THE COST OF DISCIPLESHIP (MATTHEW 16:24-27; MARK 8:34-38; LUKE 9:23-26).

Not only would Jesus experience rejection and death, His disciples would likewise have a cross of their own to carry. Jesus told His disciples and a crowd that had gathered around them that those who would follow Him had to deny themselves and bear their cross. He was warning all who believe in Him that the road of faith is not easy. It requires personal sacrifice and invites persecution. However, the path of faith in Jesus Christ leads to eternal life. "Whoever will lose his life for me and for the gospel," Jesus said, "will save it." Following Jesus is not easy, but it certainly is worth it! After all, Jesus will return in all His divine glory accompanied by the angels of heaven. He will reward everyone who has faced hardship for having followed Him.

#101—THE TRANSFIGURATION OF JESUS (MATTHEW 16:28—17:8; MARK 9:1-8; LUKE 9:27-36).

Jesus concluded His discussion with His disciples at Caesarea-Philippi by making a promise that must have captured their attention. He said that some who were standing there in His presence would not die before they had seen Him, the messianic Son of Man, come in the power of God's kingdom. In other words, some of Jesus' disciples would soon witness the splendor of God's kingdom. It's interesting to observe that Matthew, Mark, and Luke each attach their account of Jesus' transfiguration to this promise. Apparently they understood Jesus' promise that day to have been fulfilled in the splendor of the transfiguration.

Six days later Jesus took three of His disciples—Peter, James, and John—up a high mountain. The location of this event is uncertain. Plenty of time had passed for Jesus to leave the foothills of Mount Hermon and return to the hills of Galilee. Although we don't know where this event took place, we know that it changed the lives of these three disciples forever. Arriving at a secluded place with His three closest disciples, Jesus prayed. While He was praying, there was a change in Jesus' appearance. This transformation, or transfiguration, of Jesus' appearance made His face shine like the brightness of the sun. His clothes also became brilliantly white, as bright as a flash of lightning. Jesus had taken on the radiance of His divine glory identical to the fiery image of God's presence in Old Testament times. Jesus is God, and He for this moment revealed the fullness of His glory.

As the three disciples witnessed this transfiguration, they saw two men appear at Jesus' side. The Old Testament prophets Moses and Elijah were there talking with Jesus. What a conversation that must have been! They spoke about Jesus' impending departure—His sacrificial death—that would take place in Jerusalem. Just a few days earlier, Jesus had begun to reveal this aspect of His mission to His disciples. Now, Peter, James, and John heard the same truth revealed by Moses and Elijah in the presence of Jesus. Although these three disciples had been sleepy, they were now wide awake as they witnessed this brief intrusion of God's kingdom into the world.

After Moses and Elijah left, Peter spoke up. He

acknowledged the privilege it was for him and his companions to witness this event and suggested that they build three temporary shelters, or tents, in honor of Jesus, Moses, and Elijah. Mark's Gospel states that Peter didn't really know what to say in response to this remarkable revelation. His best idea seems to have been to erect at least a temporary shrine. But this suggestion was quickly eclipsed by another event. A bright cloud enveloped Jesus and the three disciples and a voice from the cloud said, "This is my beloved Son. Listen to him!" God the Father spoke audibly to the three disciples, instructing them to recognize Jesus as His unique Son and to be reverently obedient to everything Jesus had to say. It's not surprising to read that the three disciples fell to the ground in fear. But Jesus tenderly reassured them and helped them to their feet. When they looked up, they saw no one except Jesus. This amazing moment of glory had passed. Jesus had been revealed in His kingdom splendor. But there was still work to be done. So Jesus led Peter, James, and John down the mountain to rejoin the other disciples and to complete His ministry.

#102—JESUS TEACHES ABOUT ELIJAH (MATTHEW 17:9-13; MARK 9:9-13).

As Jesus was descending from the mount of transfiguration, He instructed Peter, James, and John not to tell anyone about this experience until after His resurrection. The three disciples talked among themselves about what Jesus meant by saying that He would rise from the dead. They had not yet grasped the truth of Jesus' redeeming work on the cross. These three disciples had many questions. One question related to the role of Elijah in God's kingdom plan. Having just seen Elijah on the mount of transfiguration, they posed their question to Jesus. Why, they wondered, did the teachers of the law say that Elijah had to come first? Jesus assured them that, in fulfillment of Old Testament prophecy, Elijah indeed needed to come prior to the arrival of God's kingdom. But Elijah had already come. The religious leaders didn't recognize Elijah's presence among them and he was unjustly put to death. Matthew's Gospel tells us that the disciples knew Jesus was talking about John the Baptist. As a prophet of God, John had come in the spirit and power of Elijah. He had proclaimed the nearness of God's kingdom and introduced Jesus to the world. But John had been executed by Herod Antipas, and soon Jesus too would die. As tragic as the deaths of John and Jesus were, they fit perfectly within the redemptive plan of God. God, through Jesus, was reaching into this sin filled world to rescue us from the penalty of our rebellion against Him.

#103—JESUS CASTS OUT A DIFFICULT DEMON (MATTHEW 17:14-21; MARK 9:14-29; LUKE 9:37-43).

While Jesus had been on the mount of transfiguration with Peter, James, and John, the other disciples had been busy as well. When Jesus returned to them, they were surrounded by a crowd and they were engaged in an argument with some of the religious leaders. Jesus' presence immediately calmed the situation. Jesus asked what the argument was all about.

A man in the crowd spoke up. He came, knelt before

Jesus, and explained that his son was the subject of the debate. This poor man's son was demon possessed. The demon took away the boy's ability to speak, inflicted him with seizures, made him stumble into flames or water, and in other ways caused the boy great physical harm. The desperate father had taken the boy to Jesus' disciples for help, but the disciples were powerless against this particular demon.

Jesus expressed a general rebuke to the crowd for its disbelief. He then told the man to bring the boy to Him. As the boy approached, the demon threw him into another convulsive fit. Jesus tenderly asked the father how long the boy had been tormented by this demon. The father said that this had gone on since childhood. He then asked Jesus to do something if He could. Jesus responded to the man's cautious faith by saying that anything is possible to those who believe. The boy's father replied honestly and hopefully, "I believe. Help my unbelief." Then Jesus rebuked this difficult demon, and the demon violently left the boy. The boy looked dead at first, but Jesus took his hand and helped him to his feet. The demon was gone forever. The boy was healed. He and his father must have embraced as they made their way home to a new life. Jesus had not only released the boy from his demonic torment, but had relieved the father from his faltering faith.

When His disciples were once again alone with Jesus, they asked Him why they had been unable to cast out this difficult demon. After all, Jesus had previously granted His disciples the authority to heal the sick and cast out all kinds of demons, an authority which they had exercised freely on their first mission away from Jesus. Jesus answered that, even though they had authority, they still did not have sufficient faith. If their faith was even the size of a tiny mustard seed they would be able to move mountains. But their faith was still too small. Some things are impossible apart from faith and prayer and, in some cases, fasting as well. Only through prayer can we grow in faith and in our ability to perform the works God calls us to do. The disciples had come a long way, but they still had much to learn.

⚑104—JESUS AGAIN TEACHES ABOUT HIS DEATH (MATTHEW 17:22-23; MARK 9:30-32; LUKE 9:44-45).

At this stage in His ministry, Jesus began to distance Himself from the crowds and focus on teaching His disciples. As they walked through the region of Galilee, Jesus again told His disciples that He would be betrayed, arrested, and put to death. But He assured them that He would rise again on the third day. The disciples were unable to grasp Jesus' warning, and yet were afraid to ask Him to clarify His intentions. They were also filled with grief over these conversations about Jesus' death. Hadn't Jesus come to restore God's kingdom on earth? Wasn't that the role of the Messiah? The disciples couldn't understand how Jesus' death fit into God's plan.

⚑105—JESUS PROVIDES A COIN IN A FISH'S MOUTH (MATTHEW 17:24-27).

At this point Matthew's Gospel records an almost whimsical account of one of Jesus' miracles. It's as if Matthew sensed a need to lighten the atmosphere surrounding Jesus' discussions about His impending death. Jesus and His disciples had returned to Capernaum along the shore of the Sea of Galilee. One day one of the religious leaders cornered Peter and asked if Jesus paid His share of the tax that supported the temple in Jerusalem. After all, everyone was expected to pay this tax. Peter confidently assured this representative of the temple that Jesus indeed would pay His temple tax.

When Peter arrived back at the house where Jesus was staying, Jesus initiated a conversation about the temple tax. After all, as God in the flesh, Jesus knew even the conversations that took place away from His presence. Jesus asked Peter who he thought should pay taxes. Do kings collect taxes from their children or merely from the citizens of their kingdom? Peter responded that kings only collect taxes from citizens. So, Jesus concluded, the sons of kings are exempt from taxes. By implication, Jesus as the Son of God was exempt from paying the tax supporting the house of God.

Peter was in a pickle. He had assured the temple tax collector that Jesus would pay the tax, but Jesus now stated that He was exempt from the tax. Once again Peter had spoken out of turn. But Jesus didn't want to make too much out of a harmless expectation regarding the temple tax. So He instructed Peter to go down to the Sea of Galilee and throw in a fishing line. In the mouth of the first fish he would catch Peter would find a single coin that was sufficient to pay Jesus' and Peter's share of the temple tax. Jesus had the power to guide a fish to a coin and then to guide that same fish to Peter's fishhook! Jesus also had the power to amaze His outspoken disciple with His grace.

₱106—JESUS TEACHES ON GREATNESS IN THE KINGDOM (MATTHEW 18:1-14; MARK 9:33-50; LUKE 9:46-50).

While they were in Capernaum, Jesus questioned His disciples about an argument in which they had been engaged as they walked along the road. The disciples were embarrassed because they had been arguing among themselves who would be considered greatest in God's kingdom. Instead of trying to comprehend Jesus' teachings about His death, they were debating their own personal merits. Jesus told His disciples that whoever wanted to be first must be last. He then took a small child in His arms and said that His disciples had to change and become like a child if they wanted to be great in God's kingdom. God honors humility. He honors a servant attitude. He honors those who welcome and encourage others in their faith. To welcome a child is to welcome Jesus, and to welcome Jesus is to welcome His heavenly Father. The very fact that the disciples had been arguing about greatness meant that they had not yet attained greatness. Those who are great in God's sight are not concerned about personal greatness. They're concerned about others.

At this point John spoke up. He said that they had seen a man casting out demons in Jesus' name and had rebuked the man because he was not one of the twelve apostles. Jesus said not to stop anyone who was serving in His name. If a person was not opposed to Jesus, then that person must be supportive of Him. There was no need for fine distinctions that would separate Jesus' true followers. To cause even one of Jesus' simplest followers to stumble or sin is an act worthy of judgment. Jesus said it would be better to be thrown into the sea with a millstone around one's neck than to cause one of His followers to sin. In even more extreme imagery, Jesus said that it would be better to sever a hand or foot or to pluck out an eye than to allow these members of our bodies to lead us into sin and away from faith in Him. Those who remain in their sin will be thrown into the eternal torments of hell, but those who turn away from their sin through faith in Jesus Christ will enjoy the blessings of eternal life. Jesus also said that even the simplest, childlike believers deserve our respect because they have angels representing them in the presence of God in heaven. Like a shepherd who searches for one lost sheep, leaving the ninety-nine behind, so the Father in heaven rejoices over one lost soul that comes to Him. Therefore, there is no reason to covet greatness in God's kingdom. Greatness is seen in a genuine love for others, a love that compels us to serve them and share the good news of Jesus with them.

#107—JESUS TEACHES ON CHURCH DISCIPLINE AND FORGIVENESS (MATTHEW 18:15-35).

At this point Matthew's Gospel includes an extended discourse in which Jesus describes church discipline and forgiveness. This is the second time that Jesus refers to His future community of believers known as the church.

Jesus said that if a believer sins against a fellow believer, the one who has been wronged must go to that sinning brother or sister and seek to restore their relationship. If this attempt at restoration is successful, all is well. But if the sinning believer refuses to respond, other believers are to be brought in as witnesses and attempt to restore the sinning brother or sister. If this approach to restoration is unsuccessful, the sinning believer is to be taken before the church. If the sinning brother or sister won't respond to the church's loving attempts at restoration, he or she is to be excluded from the community of believers.

There is power in the community of Jesus' followers, the church. That which is bound by the church is bound in heaven, and that which is freed by the church is freed in heaven. As with similar statements of Jesus, these words should never be used to support a divisive spirit but to show the importance of loving, prayerful restoration. Jesus also said that where two are three believers are gathered in His name, He is present among them. This means that in matters of church discipline, and in matters of church life in general, Jesus has a real presence among His followers. Our words and actions must, therefore, reflect the love, purity, and presence of Jesus.

Peter then raised a question about forgiveness, one with which we've all had to wrestle from time to time. How often must we forgive someone who keeps sinning against us? Peter suggested forgiving such a person seven times before calling it quits. Jesus, however, raised the bar as He so often did. Don't stop forgiving after seven offenses. Forgive someone seventy-seven times, or seventy times seven times! In other words, model forgiveness even as Jesus has modeled it for us.

Jesus then went on to describe forgiveness by presenting His parable of the unmerciful servant. A servant owed an enormous debt to his master, but was unable to pay off this debt. As was the custom of the day, the master ordered that the servant and his family be sold into slavery. But the servant begged for mercy, and the master graciously forgave his debt. The servant went away completely forgiven. But then the servant who had been forgiven of his enormous debt found a fellow servant who owed him a much smaller debt. The fellow servant was unable to repay his debt to the first servant. The first servant, who had been forgiven an enormous debt by his master, showed no mercy and ordered his fellow servant to be thrown into jail. When the first servant's master learned of this, he summoned this unmerciful servant and reminded him of how much he'd been forgiven. Why hadn't he who had received mercy been merciful? Then the master threw this unmerciful servant into jail. Jesus concluded this parable by saying that we who have received unlimited forgiveness from God must show unlimited forgiveness toward others.

Jesus' seventh Galilean tour had taken Him north to Caesarea-Philippi, where Peter had confessed Him as the Christ, the promised Messiah. Jesus had revealed His glory to three of His disciples on the mount of transfiguration. He had also reinforced for His disciples the fact that He must die and rise again. Jesus' work in Galilee was now done. It was time to move south again, to the region of Judea. The Great Galilean Ministry had come to a close. The day of Jesus' death was approaching. But there were still people who needed Jesus' healing touch. There were still people who needed to hear the message of hope, the good news of God's kingdom.

7

THE LATER JUDEAN AND PEREAN MINISTRY OF JESUS (PART 1)

JERUSALEM WAS THE EPICENTER OF JEWISH LIFE AND thought. Although Jesus had focused much of His ministry in the northern region of Galilee, the time had come for Him to work closer to the core of Judaism. He had begun His ministry in Judea, paralleling John the Baptist's work in the Judean wilderness. Now, Jesus returned to Judea with His disciples. He would continue to engage in an itinerant preaching ministry, this time in the villages of Judea and in the region of Perea east of the Jordan River. But Jerusalem became the focus of His attention, and it was in Jerusalem that Jesus would give His life for our sins.

Jesus' Ministry in and around Jerusalem

Jesus' Later Judean Ministry is recorded primarily in the Gospels of Luke and John. In fact, each of these Gospels contains information about Jesus' life that is found in no other Gospel. This unique material helps us to gain a greater understanding of Jesus' ministry and the events leading up to His crucifixion.

#108—JESUS RESISTS PUBLIC DISPLAYS OF HIS POWER (JOHN 7:1-10).

Jesus had remained in Galilee for an extended period of time for several reasons, including the fact that the Jewish leaders in Judea wanted to take His life. However, the fall Feast of Tabernacles was approaching. Jesus' brothers chided Him for not taking advantage of this festival period to reveal His miraculous powers. After all, the Feast of Tabernacles would provide an excellent opportunity for Jesus to gain even greater public notoriety. However, Jesus' brothers were not really interested in seeing Jesus advance in His ministry. They didn't yet believe in Him, though after the resurrection they, too, would come to believe in Him as the Messiah.

Jesus told His brothers that His time had not yet come, even though to their way of thinking, every day was the same. His brothers were not the objects of hatred. But the world hated Jesus because He spoke out against its sinful condition. So, Jesus encouraged His brothers to go to the Feast of Tabernacles without Him. However, after His brothers left for Jerusalem, Jesus went also. He did so secretly in an effort to avoid drawing undue attention.

#109—JESUS IS REJECTED IN SAMARIA (LUKE 9:51-56).

Jesus knew that the time of His death was approaching. He would have but a few short months to complete His work on earth. Luke's Gospel tells us that at this stage Jesus set out for Jerusalem resolved to accomplish His mission. As He made His way from Galilee to Jerusalem, He chose to travel through Samaria. Earlier in His ministry He had received a warm welcome by the people in the Samaritan village of Sychar. This time Jesus sent messengers ahead into another Samaritan village to prepare for His arrival. But the people of that village knew He was on His way to Jerusalem, and since the Samaritans hated their purely Jewish cousins, they counted Jesus among their enemies. These Samaritans refused to welcome Jesus. Two of Jesus' disciples, James and John, reflected the animosity between the Jews and the Samaritans of their day. They asked Jesus if they should call fire down from heaven and destroy the inhospitable Samaritan village. James and John seemed only too eager to see the Samaritans receive divine judgment. But Jesus rebuked these two disciples for their insensitivity. Instead, Jesus and His disciples traveled on to another village, presumably one that welcomed them in their midst.

#110—JESUS TEACHES ABOUT SELF-SACRIFICE (MATTHEW 8:18-22; LUKE 9:57-62).

Somewhere along their journey from Galilee to Jerusalem, Jesus and His disciples encountered three men who expressed their interest in joining the ranks of Jesus' followers. The first man, a respected scribe, promised to follow Jesus anywhere. Jesus simply pointed out to this man the rigors of His itinerant ministry. Even foxes have holes and birds have nests, Jesus told him. But Jesus had no permanent dwelling. He had no place to rest His head. The second man who encountered Jesus along the way was already among the broader group of Jesus' disciples. Jesus invited this man to follow Him more closely. The man balked, however. He asked Jesus to allow him first to go and bury his father. Jesus pointed out, as He had on other occasions, that following Him meant prioritizing our human relationships. He told the man to let the dead bury their dead. Jesus must come first even among our most cherished relationships if we are to be His disciples. The third man who came to Jesus at that time promised to be a loyal follower. However, he requested permission to first go back and bid farewell to his family. Jesus again stressed the importance of total commitment. He simply said, "No one who puts his hand on the plow and then looks back at what is behind is fit for the kingdom of God." True discipleship demands wholehearted, consistent commitment. It requires unflinching self-sacrifice.

111—JESUS TEACHES DURING THE FEAST OF TABERNACLES (JOHN 7:11-36).

In Jerusalem, the people had begun to celebrate the Feast of Tabernacles. The religious leaders were keeping an eye out for Jesus, wondering if He would attend the feast. The common people were whispering among themselves about Jesus. Some said that Jesus was a good man, while others had bought into the lies of the religious leaders and concluded that Jesus was a deceiver. No one dared say anything publicly about Jesus, however, because they feared the possible repercussions from the religious elite.

Jesus did, in fact, attend the Feast of Tabernacles, but kept His presence in Jerusalem secret for the first few days of the feast. However, halfway through the feast He went into the temple courts and began to teach publicly. The Jewish leaders were impressed with Jesus' knowledge and wondered how He had acquired such insights without having gone through the normal training processes. Jesus told them that His message and authority came from God the Father who had sent Him. He also said that anyone who truly honored God would have no trouble recognizing that His teaching came from God. Jesus spoke divine truth.

Jesus then accused the religious leaders of failing to obey God's law. He also asked them why they were trying to kill Him. The religious leaders accused Jesus of being demon possessed and denied any intention of killing Him. But Jesus wasn't duped by their false assurances. It seems that the issue of healing on the Sabbath day was still the flashpoint in the debate between Jesus and His accusers. Jesus pointed out that no one complained about circumcising an infant on the Sabbath day, so they should not be upset that Jesus had healed a man on the Sabbath day. Jesus may have been referring to His healing of the lame man near the pool of Bethesda during one of His previous visits to Jerusalem. Clearly the Jewish leaders took issue with any number of miracles that Jesus had performed on the Sabbath day.

The fact that Jesus was openly teaching in the temple

courts wasn't lost on the people of Jerusalem. Some of them began to wonder why the authorities hadn't tried to stop Him since it was well known that they wanted to put Jesus to death. Some even wondered if the religious leaders were beginning to consider Jesus as the Messiah. Still, the people expressed their doubts. After all, they believed that the origin of the Messiah would be a mystery, while they assumed they knew where Jesus came from.

Jesus acknowledged that the people did indeed know some aspects of His background. But in reality they knew very little about Jesus. They didn't realize that He was sent by God the Father in heaven. Jesus' declaration of His unique relationship with God the Father was too much for the religious leaders. They attempted to seize Him, but for some reason couldn't follow through with their intentions. Jesus' time had not yet come. As a result, many people put their faith in Jesus. They recognized that Jesus' miracles provided incontrovertible evidence for His messianic claims.

Because Jesus was gaining new followers, the Pharisees and the chief priests sent a contingent of guards to arrest Him at an opportune time during the feast. Jesus knew that His time was short. He declared to the religious leaders that He would soon leave them. At that point His enemies would look for Him but be unable to find Him. They wouldn't be able to go where He was going because of their unbelief. The religious leaders didn't understand that Jesus was talking about going back to heaven. Instead, they concluded that Jesus intended to leave Judea and travel among the dispersed Jews throughout the Roman Empire.

#112—JESUS CAUSES DIVISION AMONG THE PEOPLE AT THE FEAST OF TABERNACLES (JOHN 7:37-53).

On the final day of the Feast of Tabernacles, Jesus stood among the crowd and shouted, "If anyone thirsts, let him come to me and drink." He promised that all who put their faith in Him would experience inner, spiritual satisfaction. They would have streams of living water flowing inside. John's Gospel informs us that Jesus was referring to the future indwelling of the Holy Spirit. After Jesus' death and resurrection, He sent the Holy Spirit to live inside all true believers.

Hearing Jesus' bold declaration, many of the people concluded that Jesus was truly the promised prophet of God. Others concluded more precisely that Jesus was the Messiah. But many others remained skeptical. They wondered how the Messiah could come from Galilee when the Old Testament clearly taught that Bethlehem was to be the Messiah's hometown. After all, the Messiah had to be a descendant of David, and David was from Bethlehem. These skeptics were unaware that, while Jesus grew up in Galilee, He had been born in Bethlehem. A pronounced division grew among the Jewish people. Some saw Jesus as their Messiah. Others wanted to arrest Him. But no one was able to lay a hand on Him because His time had not yet come.

The guards whom the religious leaders had sent to arrest Jesus midway through the feast returned to the Pharisees and chief priests on the last day of the feast. When questioned why they had not fulfilled their duty, they simply responded, "No one ever spoke like this man speaks." The religious leaders were incensed. Had these guards fallen under the spell of Jesus' teachings? The Pharisees claimed that none of the religious leaders among the Jews believed in Jesus. Only the unlearned, ignorant crowd was following Him. At this point Nicodemus, who had gone to Jesus one night and learned about the new birth, defended Him. He reminded his colleagues that the law didn't condemn a man without first hearing his testimony. The rest of the religious leaders sneered at Nicodemus. They accused him of being a despised Galilean like Jesus and told him that God's promised prophet wouldn't come from that region. How little they really knew about Jesus. How eager they were to reject Jesus' offer of living water.

#113—JESUS FORGIVES A WOMAN CAUGHT IN ADULTERY (JOHN 8:1-11).

After the Feast of Tabernacles came to an end, it appears that Jesus remained in Jerusalem for several weeks. John 8:1-11 provides an account of an event that took place the day after the close of the feast. While many ancient manuscripts don't include this account, it does reflect what we know of Jesus' wisdom, love, and forgiveness. Jesus returned to the temple courts. This setting provided an appropriate place for Him to carry out His public preaching ministry. As people gathered around Him, Jesus began to teach. Then the Pharisees and the teachers of the law brought before Jesus a woman who had been caught in the sin of adultery. They pointed out to Jesus that the law required that she be put to death by stoning. What did Jesus have to say regarding this case? If Jesus endorsed stoning this woman He would bring on the wrath of the Roman authorities, who alone could enforce the death penalty. Furthermore, to insist on this woman's execution for her sin would run contrary to Jesus' message of love and forgiveness. But to deny the requirements of the law would prove to the crowd that Jesus was not a prophet of God. Obviously, this was a trap. The religious leaders hoped to back Jesus into a corner and discredit Him completely.

Jesus paused and, with His finger, began to write in the sand on the ground in front of Him. Our curiosity forces us to ask an unanswerable question. What was Jesus writing? Was He recording scripture verses about forgiveness? Was He rewriting the law? Unfortunately, His written words were soon erased by the trampling feet of the crowd. The Pharisees demanded an answer. Should this sinful woman be stoned to death? Jesus then gave this profound reply. "Let him who is without sin cast the first stone at her." He then continued to write on the ground. Those who had accused the woman began to slowly walk away. When all had left, Jesus looked up again and spoke to the adulterous woman. He asked what had become of her accusers. None was left to condemn her. Without witnesses to condemn her, the woman was free. So Jesus told the woman that He didn't condemn her either. He never condoned her sin, but He was more interested in forgiving her than judging her. He said to the adulterous woman, "Go and sin no longer." Christ's forgiveness prompts us to forsake further sin. This woman went away forgiven and, presumably, changed forever.

¶114—JESUS TEACHES ABOUT HIS PURPOSE AND DEITY (JOHN 8:12-59).

As Jesus was teaching in the temple courts He declared to the gathered crowd, "I am the light of the world." He claimed to possess the light that gives eternal life. This statement initiated yet another debate with the Pharisees. These self-righteous leaders accused Jesus of presenting an invalid testimony. He was merely making claims about Himself without providing adequate supporting witnesses. Jesus responded by defending His personal testimony about Himself. After all, He had been sent by God the Father. Jesus and His heavenly Father constituted the two witnesses that were necessary to verify a claim.

Even though tensions were growing, no one dared to arrest Jesus because, once again, His time had not yet come. Only when the time was right would Jesus go to the cross. In fact, Jesus went on to tell the Pharisees that He would eventually go away, and without Him they would die in their sins. The Pharisees, always eager to assume the worst, wondered if Jesus intended to kill Himself. Jesus continued His main thought by saying that all who refused to believe in Him would die in their sins. Soon, Jesus warned, the Pharisees would "lift up" the Son of Man, referring to His being lifted up on a cross. Even then, Jesus would be fulfilling the plan of the One who had sent Him. As Jesus spoke about His impending death, some of the people put their faith in Him. He assured these new followers that, if they would abide in His teachings, they would know the truth and that truth would set them free.

Jesus' opponents picked up on His promise of

freedom. They said that they were Abraham's descendants and had never been slaves to anyone. Had they forgotten the bondage of the Israelites in Egypt, their captivity in Babylon, or their current subjection to the Roman Empire? However, Jesus wasn't talking about political freedom. He was describing freedom of the heart, freedom from sin. Jesus alone could grant this kind of freedom because of His divine relationship with God the Father.

The Jewish leaders claimed that Abraham was their father. Jesus countered by saying that if Abraham was their true spiritual father, they would have no difficulty in accepting Him as their Messiah. The Pharisees then accused Jesus of being an illegitimate child. His lineage was suspect in their minds. In contrast, they now claimed that God was their true Father. Again, Jesus told His accusers that if God was truly their Father, they would accept and love Him because He came from God the Father. Instead of being God's children, those who rejected Jesus were Satan's offspring.

The Pharisees then accused Jesus of being a demon possessed Samaritan. Jesus denied such a preposterous accusation, and said that those who follow Him will never see death. The Jewish leaders thought they had at last trapped Jesus. Jesus claimed to be able to prevent death, yet Abraham and all the ancient prophets had died. His claim, they concluded, was ridiculous. Jesus responded by saying that Abraham looked forward to seeing His day and rejoiced when it came. The Jewish leaders pointed out that Jesus wasn't even fifty years old. How could He have seen Abraham? Then Jesus made an unmistakable claim to His eternal existence as God. He said, "Before

Abraham was, I am!" At this the Jewish leaders picked up stones, ready to stone Jesus to death. But Jesus slipped away, avoiding their evil intentions. His time had not yet come. Still, Jesus had effectively declared His divine nature, His saving mission, and His life-giving power.

#115—JESUS HEALS A MAN BORN BLIND (JOHN 9:1-41).

As Jesus was walking along He encountered a man who had been born blind. The disciples asked what we may have wondered at times when we see someone in a tragic situation. Why did this happen? Was it a result of sin? The disciples asked Jesus if the blind man or one of his parents had sinned, thereby bringing on his blindness. Jesus assured His disciples that this man's blindness was not a result of sin, but had a grander purpose. God can be glorified in every circumstance. Then Jesus spit on the ground to make some mud and applied the mud to the man's eyes. He then instructed the man to go to the Pool of Siloam, south of the temple area in Jerusalem, and wash his eyes. When the man had done so, he could see perfectly!

The man who had been healed of his blindness went home. His friends and neighbors were amazed and asked how it was that he could now see. The man said that Jesus had healed him. The man's friends presented the man to the Pharisees, but the Pharisees took offense at the man's miraculous healing because it had taken place on the Sabbath day. They told the man that Jesus wasn't from God. But others who were present asked how a sinner could perform such a miraculous sign. Again, the people were divided over the identity of Jesus.

The Pharisees finally turned to the blind man and asked his opinion. The man simply stated that he believed Jesus was a prophet. He must have come from God. Jesus' skeptics continued to doubt Jesus' identity and the blind man's testimony. They called in the man's parents, who assured them that their son had been born blind. They could not account for his healing. Neither did they dare to oppose the Pharisees. After all, the Pharisees had made it known that anyone who acknowledged Jesus as the promised Messiah would be kicked out of the synagogue, isolated from the spiritual and social life of Judaism. This was no small penalty.

The Pharisees went back to the formerly blind man and assured him that Jesus was a sinful man. The man replied that he didn't know if Jesus was or wasn't a sinner. He only knew that Jesus had healed him. He once was blind, but now he could see. When the Pharisees persisted in questioning the man, he asked them if they wanted to join him in becoming a disciple of Jesus. The Pharisees were outraged. They insulted the man and claimed to be disciples of Moses, not Jesus. After all, they didn't even know where Jesus came from, so how could they follow Him? The man expressed his amazement at the Pharisees' ignorance of Jesus' origin given His miraculous power. The Pharisees, totally frustrated at this point, rebuked the man for trying to instruct them in religious matters and severed him from all relationship with the synagogue.

Jesus quickly learned about the Pharisees' pathetic reaction to the blind man's healing. He found the man and asked him if he believed in the Messiah. The man, having never seen Jesus with his eyes, asked who the Messiah was. Jesus said, in essence, "You're looking at Him." The man expressed verbally his faith in Jesus and worshiped Him on the spot. Jesus declared that He had come to give sight to all who are blind spiritually. Some Pharisees heard this statement and asked if Jesus thought they were blind. Jesus replied that if they were blind, they would not be guilty of sin. But because they thought they could see, they were still trapped in their sins. It's one thing to be blind. It's yet another to recognize our spiritual blindness and turn by faith to Jesus.

116—JESUS TEACHES ABOUT THE GOOD SHEPHERD (JOHN 10:1-21).

Earlier Jesus had described Himself as the light of the world. Now He presented a brief discourse in which He called Himself the gate to life and the good shepherd. Jesus told His audience that only the shepherd enters a sheepfold by way of the gate. Thieves climb over the wall, but the shepherd goes through the gate. The shepherd leads his sheep, calling them by name. The shepherd shows intimate care for his sheep. Because the people didn't understand what Jesus was driving at, He went on to explain this imagery.

Jesus said that He is the gate for the sheep. Those who put their faith in Him enter into life. They have free access to God's protective fold and His plush pastures. Thieves, those who reject Jesus, only intend to inflict damage on the sheep. Jesus came to give His sheep, the true people of God, eternal and abundant life.

Jesus then shifted His analogy, calling Himself the

good shepherd. As the good shepherd, Jesus came to sacrifice His life for the sake of His sheep. As the good shepherd, Jesus knows His sheep intimately, and they know Him. Jesus would bring all of God's people, even those from different sheepfolds, into His flock. He would willingly lay down His life for His sheep, and He would then take up His life again through the resurrection.

Once again the people were divided in their opinion about Jesus. Some claimed that He was demon possessed. Others said that His words warranted a different conclusion. They even cited Jesus' healing of the blind man in favor of supporting His divine claims. These sheep were hearing Jesus' voice and recognized Him. Even today many people fail to recognize Jesus as their shepherd and savior. But many have heard His voice and are following Him.

#117—JESUS SENDS OUT THE SEVENTY-TWO DISCIPLES (LUKE 10:1-24).

Jesus had many followers. Some, particularly the twelve apostles, were very close to Him. Others composed a wider circle of disciples who were also highly committed to Jesus. Jesus selected seventy-two (some manuscripts say seventy) men from this extended group of disciples to perform a special mission. As He had previously sent out the twelve to preach the gospel in Galilee, now He sent out the seventy-two throughout the towns and villages of Judea. Two by two, these evangelists went out to carry Jesus' message.

Jesus instructed these messengers to pray for even more workers because the harvest was plentiful but the workers were few in number. He warned them to be on guard because they would be like lambs among wolves. They were not to take provisions, or be delayed along the way. Instead, they were to go into each village, find a hospitable home, and stay with that family until their work in that village was done. They were to preach a simple message, proclaiming, "The kingdom of God is near!" Those who rejected this message would face God's judgment because they were, in fact, rejecting Jesus and rejecting the Father in heaven who had sent Jesus.

When the seventy-two returned from their itinerant preaching ministry, they acknowledged that even the demons submitted to them in Jesus' name. Jesus rejoiced with them in their spiritual victories, and reminded them to find their greatest joy in the fact that their names are recorded forever in heaven. Jesus then prayed, giving praise to God the Father for revealing His spiritual truths to simple, childlike hearts. Having offered praise to the Father, Jesus turned to the seventy-two disciples and pronounced a blessing on them for their work. They had advanced the proclamation of God's kingdom and prepared the road for Jesus' final months of ministry.

#118—JESUS GIVES THE PARABLE OF THE GOOD SAMARITAN (LUKE 10:25-37).

Everywhere, Jesus faced resistance to His message. An expert in the Old Testament law approached Jesus one day and tested Jesus with a very basic question. He asked what he needed to do to inherit eternal life. Jesus, knowing that this man was well versed in the law, asked him what the law taught. The man responded that he was to love God with his whole heart and to love his neighbor as himself. Jesus said that the man had answered correctly. But the legal expert was looking for a loophole. He asked Jesus, "Who is my neighbor?" In other words, how far must my love extend in order for God to accept me?

Jesus then told the parable of the Good Samaritan. In this parable, a man who was traveling from Jerusalem to Jericho was accosted by thieves along the way. The thieves beat the man, stole his belongings, and left him to die. A priest, highly respected within Jewish circles, came across this man but ignored his plight and passed by on the other side of the road. A Levite, another man of great honor, did likewise. But then along came a Samaritan. The Jews despised the Samaritans. But in the parable this Samaritan took pity on the beaten victim. He bandaged the man's wounds, put the man on his donkey, and took the man to a nearby inn. There, the Samaritan paid the innkeeper for the man's expenses during his recovery and promised further remuneration if needed.

Having told this parable, Jesus asked the legal expert, who was trying to justify his apparent lack of love, to identify the true neighbor in the story. The legal expert correctly identified the Samaritan, the man who had showed mercy. Only the Samaritan had acted like a neighbor to the man in need. Jesus told the legal expert to go and do the same thing. Loving our neighbor means helping those who have a need regardless of any practical inconveniences or perceived differences.

#119—JESUS STAYS AT THE HOME OF MARY AND MARTHA (LUKE 10:38-42).

In addition to His traveling disciples, Jesus had developed a network of followers in various towns throughout Galilee and Judea. One family that opened its home to Jesus and His disciples was that of a woman named Martha and her sister Mary. These two women were deeply committed to Jesus, yet showed their devotion in completely different ways. Mary was mesmerized by Jesus' teachings, and sat listening to Him while her sister Martha went about taking care of serving the guests. Eventually Martha went to Jesus and asked Him to tell Mary to help her in her work. Jesus lovingly said, "Martha, Martha, you are anxious and upset about many things." The most important thing in life wasn't taking care of physical needs but spiritual needs. Mary, Jesus said, had chosen the better way, and He refused to take her away from her personal soul search. Mary's example reminds us that we're to take time to sit at Jesus' feet, to learn from His Word, and to develop our spiritual walk with Him. Then we will be better prepared to serve Him.

8

THE LATER JUDEAN AND PEREAN MINISTRY OF JESUS (PART 2)

JESUS HAD INTENTIONALLY RELOCATED HIS MINISTRY from Galilee to Judea. Jerusalem became the center of His work for a number of weeks following the fall Feast of Tabernacles. Eventually, Jesus would preach in some of the outlying villages of Judea and travel as far as Perea on the east side of the Jordan River. This relocation of His ministry to the southern region of Judea and its surrounding communities was a prelude to His later, climactic ministry and crucifixion in Jerusalem.

Jesus' Ministry in and around Jerusalem (Continued)

Having made Jerusalem, for the time being, His base of operations, Jesus continued to perform miracles, teach His followers, and challenge the religious authorities in and around this center of Judaism.

#120—JESUS TEACHES HIS DISCIPLES ABOUT PRAYER (LUKE 11:1-13).

Prayer was a prominent part of Jesus' ministry. He modeled a life of prayer and taught His followers how to pray. On one occasion, after Jesus had been engaged in a time of personal prayer, His disciples asked Him to teach them how to pray. Jesus outlined a pattern of prayer nearly identical to the one He had earlier presented to the crowd at the time of His Sermon on the Mount. Prayer, Jesus taught, should be addressed to God the Father who is perfectly holy in character. We're to acknowledge in prayer our desire for God's kingdom to come in fullness into this world, implying that we also want God to reign in our hearts day by day. Jesus invites us to ask God to meet our needs, including our daily need for bread and our ongoing need for forgiveness of sins. In seeking God's forgiveness through prayer, we must remember that God expects us to forgive others. Jesus also indicated that we shouldn't be content simply to have our sins forgiven, but should also seek to resist temptation by God's help.

After presenting this basic model of prayer, Jesus gave His parable of the persistent friend. He said that a man went to his friend at midnight asking to borrow bread to feed a guest who had arrived at his home. The friend was reluctant to get out of bed at such a late hour to help. He gave the excuse that the door was locked, the children were in bed, and it was inconvenient for him to get up and help out his friend at such an inconvenient hour. However, the man persisted in his request, so his friend finally got up and gave him all he needed. Jesus said that our prayer life should be like the request of the persistent friend. We should keep on praying, even when the answer doesn't appear to be forthcoming. In fact, Jesus promised, "Ask and it will be given to you. Seek and you will find. Knock and it will be opened for you." He assured us that God the Father answers our persistent prayers.

Jesus then went on to describe the goodness of God in relationship to our prayers. He said that when children ask for something to satisfy their hunger—a fish or an egg for example—fathers don't respond cruelly by giving them a snake or a scorpion instead. Even earthly fathers, who have evil, sin-stained hearts, can give good gifts to their children. Therefore, we can be sure that our heavenly Father will give good gifts to His children in response to their requests. Jesus promised that God would even give us His Holy Spirit to meet our deepest needs. God is good beyond our comprehension, and He eagerly desires to bestow His good gifts on us in answer to our prayers.

#121—JESUS DELIVERS ANOTHER DEMON POSSESSED MAN WHO WAS MUTE (LUKE 11:14-36).

Jesus once again encountered a man who was demon possessed. This demon inflicted its victim with an inability to speak. After Jesus drove out the demon, the man could once again speak, much to the amazement of the crowd. This event brought on yet another round of accusations against Jesus on the part of the religious leaders. They again accused Jesus of operating under the power of Beelzebub. Some of His opponents tested Jesus by asking Him to perform a miraculous sign.

Jesus must have become weary of these worn out accusations. He assured His accusers that Satan would not work against himself. Jesus wasn't working in cooperation with Satan. Instead, He was able to cast out demons because of the power of God. Jesus' accusers should have concluded that God's kingdom was advancing among them. However, anyone who didn't stand with Jesus clearly stood against Him. There is no middle ground in God's kingdom work. Jesus warned that an evil spirit that leaves someone may return. If that person hasn't filled his or her life with something more substantial—presumably a faith relationship with God—the evil spirit will reinvade that person's life and even bring along more evil spirits. It's not enough for us to try to empty our lives of sin. We must fill our lives with Jesus!

At this point a woman in the crowd shouted out words of blessing on Jesus' mother. Certainly Jesus had brought great honor to His mother based on the works He performed and the words He spoke. But Jesus responded to this declaration of praise for Mary by stating that God's true blessing rested on all who hear and obey God's Word. Mary had a special place in God's plan, but she was not to be honored above others who likewise fulfilled God's will for their lives.

The crowd was again growing, and Jesus continued to speak out against the false accusations of the religious leaders. He had not been operating with Satan's power, and He would grant no special sign to those who were willfully resistant to His work. Only a wicked generation would demand more signs. Once again Jesus said that the only sign He would give to confirm His message was the sign of the prophet Jonah. Jonah had been in the belly of the fish for three days and nights, and Jesus would be in the belly of the earth three days and nights before rising from the dead. Jesus went on to warn the generation of His day that they stood in the path of severe divine judgment. After all, the Queen of Sheba had gone to great lengths to hear Solomon's wisdom. Jesus was greater than Solomon, yet the people of Jesus' day refused to listen to His message. The people of Nineveh had repented when Jonah preached. Jesus was greater than Jonah, yet the people of Jesus' day refused to repent when they heard His message.

Jesus described His message as light that penetrates the darkness of the human heart. This light shouldn't be hidden from view. Jesus also said that our eyes are the lamp of our bodies, revealing whether or not there is light or darkness in our hearts. If we view Jesus' work as He claimed it to be, the saving work of God, we have spiritual light. But if we deny His claim to be our God and Savior, we are still in spiritual darkness. Jesus had made a mute man speak. He wanted to make blind hearts see.

#122—JESUS DENOUNCES RITUALISM IN THE HOME OF A PHARISEE (LUKE 11:37-54).

After Jesus finished defending Himself once again, a Pharisee invited Him for dinner. When Jesus took His place at the Pharisee's table, the Pharisee was disturbed to see that Jesus didn't first engage in the normal ritual washings. Jesus knew exactly what His host was thinking. He accused the Pharisees of washing the outside of their dishes, but neglecting the more important, inner issues of the heart. These religious leaders, though they had clean hands, had hearts that were full of greed and wickedness. They were meticulous in giving one-tenth of even their smallest herbs to God, but failed to demonstrate justice and genuine love for God. They craved the seats of honor in the synagogues, but were as spiritually dead as an unmarked grave.

One of the teachers of the law was present, and told Jesus that these accusations against the Pharisees spilled over to people of his class as well. Jesus agreed, accusing the legal experts that they were eager to load people down with all kinds of ritualistic burdens without lifting a finger to truly help them. They had built ornate tombs to honor the ancient prophets, but it was their forefathers who had killed these prophets. As experts in the law, they possessed the key to knowledge but had themselves refused to enter into the true knowledge of God and had blocked the way for others to enter in.

These accusations against the Pharisees and the teachers of the law only fueled their hatred for Jesus. Their antagonism intensified. They bombarded Jesus with questions, attempting to find a weakness in His teachings and thereby an excuse to discredit Him or even put Him to death.

¶123—Jesus Teaches about Hypocrisy, Greed, and the Coming Kingdom (Luke 12:1-59).

Crowds continued to gather around Jesus. Luke's Gospel tells us that one such crowd numbered in the thousands! On that occasion Jesus launched one of His most caustic attacks on the religious elite. He described the Pharisees as hypocrites whose teachings had spread like yeast in a batch of dough. Jesus went on to assure His followers that they need not fear these hypocritical religious leaders. After all, the religious elite could at most take away a person's life. They had no power over a person's soul. God knows our needs. He knows the minutest details of our lives, and cares for us more than we can imagine. Therefore, we should never hesitate to acknowledge our commitment to Jesus Christ. Jesus warned His followers that they would be dragged before religious councils, but promised that God would give them the necessary words to speak in their defense.

As Jesus was teaching, someone in the crowd asked Him to settle a family dispute regarding a contested inheritance. Jesus responded to the man's request by saying that He hadn't come as a judge to settle disputes. Then, sensing the man's true heart, He warned the crowd to guard against greed in its many expressions. Jesus went on to present His parable of the rich fool. The rich man in this parable produced an abundant crop and determined to build bigger barns to horde his wealth. The man was putting his confidence in his possessions. But that very night the rich man died and was called to give an account of his life before God. The rich fool's wealth had no eternal benefits. We must devote our lives, not to hording personal wealth, but to investing in that which will last for eternity.

Jesus taught His followers to depend on God rather than wealth. After all, life is defined in terms far greater than monetary measures. Furthermore, God takes care of His people. He takes care of the birds, feeding them. He takes care of the flowers in the field, clothing them in finer splendor than Solomon's robes. Therefore, God's people need not worry since God cares for us much more than He does for birds or flowers. Unbelievers spend their entire lives worrying about such material things. But we're to seek God's kingdom as our highest priority. God will take care of the rest.

Jesus, addressing His followers as His "little flock," assured them that God had granted His kingdom to them. They could confidently invest their lives in His kingdom by helping the poor and needy. God would honor their commitment. Through His parable of the prepared servants, Jesus instructed His followers to be ready to serve God at every moment. Like friends waiting for the return of the bridegroom before heading to the wedding feast, we're to be prepared at all times for the return of our Lord.

Peter then asked Jesus if these words were intended just for the immediate circle of disciples or for everyone. Jesus responded indirectly, presenting His parable of the wise and faithful manager. A wise household manager honors his master's will, taking good care of his master's servants and business affairs. The master honors such a wise household manager with greater responsibilities. But if a manager becomes lax while his master is away the master will eventually punish him. Jesus was saying to Peter that everyone has a role to play in God's kingdom. Some will be wise in their response to Jesus, while others, who are foolish, will face punishment. He went on to say that He had not come to bring peace on the earth, but fire and division. His mission wasn't to patch up a broken system but to redeem a sinful world. Some people would respond favorably to His message, while others would reject Him and oppose those who followed Him.

Jesus finished this discourse by again turning His sights on the hypocrites in the crowd. These people seemed to know how to read weather patterns, but couldn't read the signs of God's kingdom. The time had come to get right with God. Soon it would be too late.

#124—JESUS TEACHES ABOUT REPENTANCE (LUKE 13:1-9).

While Jesus was teaching the crowd, some people told Him about a tragic incident. Pontius Pilate, the Roman governor over Judea who would eventually become involved in Jesus' trial and crucifixion, had at some point murdered a group of Galileans. This crime had apparently taken place at a time when these Galileans were making sacrifices to God. We know nothing more about the details of this incident, although we do know from history that Pilate was no friend of the Jewish people.

Jesus asked what the common opinion was regarding these Galilean victims. Were they worse sinners than other people, thereby bringing on themselves a tragic death? No, Jesus assured His listeners. Everyone will eventually die, and unless we repent we must die in our sins. Jesus then referred to eighteen men who had died when a tower in the city of Siloam fell on them. These men were no more sinful than anyone else. Death comes in many ways. Everyone, not just victims of political crimes or natural disasters, will die. But in order to prevent eternal death we must repent.

Jesus then told a parable about a fruitless tree. A man planted a tree, but even after three years the tree bore no fruit. So the man ordered his servant to cut the tree down. The servant asked the man to allow him to tend and fertilize the tree for one more year. If it still didn't bear fruit, he would then cut it down. Jesus was warning the crowd that the time of judgment for sin was near, but there was still time to show fruit of repentance.

#125—JESUS HEALS A CRIPPLED WOMAN ON THE SABBATH (LUKE 13:10-17).

On a certain Sabbath day Jesus was teaching in one of the synagogues. A woman was present who had been crippled by an evil spirit for eighteen years. Jesus called the woman forward and freed her from her condition. The woman was at last able to stand up straight. She immediately offered praise to God for her healing. But the leader of the synagogue warned the people not to seek healing on the Sabbath day. He viewed such activity as a violation of God's law. As Jesus had done before, He defended miraculous healings that took place on the Sabbath day. He said that everyone unties an ox or donkey and leads it to water on the Sabbath. Shouldn't a crippled woman be blessed by being freed from her condition on the Sabbath day? Jesus' opponents were humiliated by this only-too-sensible approach, but the common people were thrilled with what Jesus was doing among them.

#126—JESUS REPEATS HIS PARABLES OF THE MUSTARD SEED AND THE YEAST (LUKE 13:18-21).

It only makes sense that Jesus, because of the itinerant nature of His ministry, would teach certain lessons or parables on more than one occasion. While Jesus was preaching in and around Jerusalem, He repeated for this new audience His parables of the mustard seed and the yeast. He said that the kingdom of God is like a tiny mustard seed that grows into a plant large enough to serve as a home to the birds of the air. The kingdom of God is also like yeast that spreads throughout a large batch of dough. Although Jesus' gospel message had a small beginning, it would grow and spread throughout the world.

#127—JESUS TEACHES ABOUT HIS DEITY AT THE FEAST OF DEDICATION (JOHN 10:22-39).

John's Gospel provides a chronological clue in understanding the extent of Jesus' ministry in and around Jerusalem. Jesus left Galilee for Jerusalem at the time of the fall Feast of Tabernacles. He apparently stayed in the vicinity of Jerusalem until the Jewish Feast of Dedication, known today as Hanukkah, in early winter. Therefore, Jesus was active in and around Jerusalem for about three months. By the time of Pentecost the following spring, Jesus would be rejected, crucified, and raised from the dead.

At the time of the Feast of Dedication, Jesus was once again teaching in the temple courts in Jerusalem. The Jewish leaders approached Jesus and demanded that He answer a question about His identity. Was He the Christ, the promised Messiah? Jesus had consistently made messianic claims. His message was clear. But His opponents refused to listen. Jesus said that His miracles and His words spoke on His behalf. However, only Jesus' true sheep would listen to His voice. Jesus declared that He gives His sheep eternal life. No once can snatch His sheep from His caring hands, nor can anyone snatch His sheep from the hands of God the Father. Jesus then made a bold declaration of His deity, saying, "I and the Father are one."

The Jewish leaders immediately recognized the magnitude of Jesus' statement. They picked up stones to kill Jesus for claiming to be God. Jesus defended His claim to deity by pointing to His miracles. But the Jewish leaders refused to recognize Jesus as God in the flesh. They said that Jesus was a mere man who blasphemously claimed to be God. Jesus cited Psalm 82:6, which refers to human rulers as gods in a limited sense of political and military authority. He then asked why His opponents should be surprised that He, the one who is truly God in the flesh, should call Himself the Son of God. After all, Jesus is one with the Father. He is in the Father, and the Father is in Him. The Jewish leaders again tried to seize Jesus since He had not backed down in the least from His claim to be God. However, Jesus slipped away unharmed. He would leave Jerusalem for a period of time, waiting until the time was right for Him to offer His life as a sacrifice for our sins.

Jesus' Ministry in and around Perea

Perea was the geo-political region east of the Jordan River. While it was close to Jerusalem, it was also ruled by a different political entity. A specially appointed Roman military governor controlled Jerusalem and its surrounding region of Judea. Perea, however, like Galilee, was under the rule of the local tyrant king Herod Antipas.

#128—JESUS WITHDRAWS TO PEREA (JOHN 10:40-42).

Herod was no friend of Jesus. In fact, it was this same Herod who had previously executed Jesus' forerunner, John the Baptist. However, in Perea Jesus would be out of the reach of Jerusalem's religious leaders who sought to take His life prematurely. Therefore, Jesus left Jerusalem and crossed the Jordan River into Perea. This was the same area where John the Baptist had carried on much of his early ministry. In the weeks between the winter Feast of Dedication and the spring Passover when He would die on the cross, Jesus ministered to the people in and around Perea. There, He healed the sick and proclaimed the good news of God's kingdom. There in Perea, many of the people put their faith in Jesus.

129—JESUS TEACHES ABOUT ENTERING THE KINGDOM (LUKE 13:22-35).

Ultimately, Jesus would return to Jerusalem. But for the time being, Jesus traveled through the towns and villages of Perea teaching the people the truths of God. At one village a man asked Jesus if only a few people would be saved. What was the scope of the gospel message? Jesus answered by challenging the crowd to intentionally pursue a relationship with God rather than leave their eternal destinies to chance. He said that the door to eternal life is indeed narrow and many will fail to enter it before the door is shut forever. Those outside will then knock on the door and plead to enter. But at that point it will be too late. Jesus warned that in the day of judgment there will be weeping and gnashing of teeth because many will be excluded from God's eternal kingdom. Still, many people from many different lands will take their places in that kingdom. The door remains open to all who will come to God through faith in Jesus Christ.

While Jesus was teaching, some Pharisees approached Him and warned Him to leave that region. They claimed that Herod Antipas wanted to kill Jesus. Jesus was undaunted by this idle threat. He instructed the Pharisees to tell Herod, whom He called "that fox," that He would continue to minister in that region until His work was done. Jesus wasn't worried about Herod. He knew that He must die in Jerusalem, not in Herod's territory. Jesus then lamented over Jerusalem. Although Jerusalem had been the place of martyrdom for many of God's prophets, Jesus still loved this city and longed to draw its inhabitants into His loving care. However, because Jerusalem rejected

Jesus it would experience divine judgment. Not until a much later day, the day of His return, will Jerusalem embrace Jesus as its blessed Savior.

⏸130—Jesus Heals a Man with Dropsy (Luke 14:1-6).

On one Sabbath day Jesus accepted an invitation to eat in the home of a prominent Pharisee. While sharing this meal together, those in the Pharisee's home were watching Jesus carefully. One of the dinner guests was a man who suffered from a disease called dropsy. This disease appears to have been characterized by severe and painful physical swelling. During the course of the meal Jesus raised a question. Was it right to heal a man on the Sabbath? No one answered. So Jesus took hold of the afflicted man, healed him, and sent him away. He then turned to the other dinner guests and reminded them that they would without hesitation help a hurting animal on the Sabbath day. The implication was obvious. Why would they help an animal on the Sabbath and oppose helping a human being? No one said anything in response to Jesus' statement or miracle. Their silence spoke for them. They were clearly not ready to rejoice in Jesus' works.

⏸131—Jesus Gives His Parable of the Seats at the Feast (Luke 14:7-14).

Apparently during this same meal at the home of the prominent Pharisee, Jesus observed how each of the guests chose for themselves the seats of honor. So Jesus told a parable to counteract their pride. He instructed His fellow guests, when invited to a wedding feast, not to take the seats of honor. After all, someone more honorable may arrive at the feast and be given the first guest's seat. The first guest would thereby be publicly humiliated. Instead, Jesus taught His listeners to take the lowest seat first. The host may then elevate that guest to a higher seat, publicly honoring that guest. Jesus then summarized His parable, saying, "For whoever exalts himself will be humbled, and whoever humbles himself will be exalted." God honors true humility.

Jesus then instructed His host not to simply invite wealthy friends and relatives to his feasts. Such a practice would only force these guests to return the favor, implying that the host may have merely been seeking his own honor by inviting honorable guests. Instead Jesus instructed His host and the others at the table to invite the poor, the crippled, the lame, and the blind to their feasts. These guests would be in no position to repay their host, and the host would experience greater blessings by having helped these hurting, needy people. Jesus also assured His host that by inviting needy people to his feasts he would be repaid with true riches in eternity.

#132—JESUS GIVES HIS PARABLE OF THE GREAT BANQUET (LUKE 14:15-24).

One of the guests at the dinner table, having listened to Jesus' instructions about seats of honor at banquets, pronounced a blessing on those who will eat at God's kingdom feast. Jesus redirected this sentiment by describing the nature of those who will be present at that future feast. In the form of a parable, Jesus described a man who invited many of his friends to attend a great banquet. Rather than accepting the man's invitation, these friends gave a variety of excuses for not participating in this banquet. One had to go examine a field that he had purchased. Another had to inspect some newly acquired cattle. Yet another had recently been married and couldn't leave his domestic responsibilities. The host became angry at his friends for rejecting his invitation with such insubstantial excuses. However, the banquet was already prepared. The man, therefore, sent his servant out to invite the poor, the crippled, the blind, and the lame to attend his banquet. Still there was room. So the man again sent his servant throughout the countryside to invite everyone to the feast. Those who had rejected the man's earlier invitation would not have a seat at the banquet. But those who accepted his invitation, no matter what their station in life, would enjoy this celebration. God has invited people from all walks of life to enter into His kingdom. Many offer excuses for rejecting God's invitation, and thereby exclude themselves from God's eternal kingdom. But all who accept His invitation through faith in Jesus Christ will enjoy eternal life with God.

#133—JESUS TEACHES ABOUT COUNTING THE COST OF DISCIPLESHIP (LUKE 14:25-35).

While Jesus was traveling throughout Perea, large crowds followed Him. He often taught these followers about the rigors of true discipleship. To be a disciple of Jesus means making Him the priority of our lives. Our other relationships must seem like hatred in comparison to our love for Christ. That's why Jesus said that following

Him means that we must hate our parents, spouse, siblings, children, and even our own lives. We must be willing to carry our own cross—the burdens that are a part of our obedience to Jesus Christ—if we want to be one of His disciples.

Jesus also instructed His followers to count the cost of discipleship. He illustrated this principle by describing a man who plans to build a tower. If the builder doesn't count the cost in advance, he may be unable to complete the project and thereby become the object of ridicule. Jesus also illustrated the importance of counting the cost of discipleship by describing a king who plans to wage war with a neighboring country. The king should measure the strength of his army before going into battle. If his troops are inadequate to win the battle, the king should seek terms of peace instead. Likewise, those who want to follow Jesus must measure the cost of discipleship. Jesus said that we must "give up everything" if we truly want to be His disciples.

Jesus then compared our lives to salt. As His disciples, our lives must stand out in an otherwise ungodly society. If we lose our spiritual influence by growing lax in our faith, we become useless to God's work on earth. We must count the cost of discipleship, including our long term commitment to follow Jesus. Discipleship cannot be a hobby. It must become an all-encompassing way of life.

134—JESUS GIVES HIS PARABLE OF THE LOST SHEEP (LUKE 15:1-7).

Jesus' message rang well with many of the spiritually disenfranchised people of His day. Tax collectors and those who were otherwise considered to be "sinners" in the eyes of the pompous Pharisees flocked to Jesus. Predictably, the Pharisees and teachers of the law complained among themselves that Jesus would welcome and even eat with such spiritually unacceptable people. Jesus, of course, knew what the religious leaders were saying about His association with sinners. In order to set the record straight, Jesus told three parables about something valuable that had been lost but was eventually found. God rejoices when lost people—tax collectors and sinners of all brands—are reunited with Him.

The first of these three parables involved a shepherd. The shepherd who has one hundred sheep and loses one doesn't abandon the lost sheep. He leaves the ninety-nine behind while he goes out searching for that lost lamb. When the shepherd finds his lost sheep, he puts it on his shoulders, takes it back home, gathers his friends and neighbors, and rejoices. That which was lost has been found. Jesus then said that there is more rejoicing in heaven over a lost sinner who repents than over ninety-nine righteous people who do not need to repent. Jesus wasn't saying that there are some people who do not need to repent. He was contrasting the lost tax collectors and sinners to the self-righteous Pharisees who didn't sense a need to repent. We are all lost and in need of repentance.

#135—JESUS GIVES HIS PARABLE OF THE LOST COIN (LUKE 15:8-10).

In His second parable, Jesus describes a woman who loses a valuable coin. This coin may have been a part of the woman's wedding dowry, and its loss would have been a source of immeasurable anxiety. Although the woman still possessed nine coins, she lit a lamp, swept the entire house, and searched carefully until she found the lost coin. When she recovered the lost coin the woman called her friends together to rejoice with her. Jesus then said that the angels of heaven rejoice when one lost sinner repents.

₱136—JESUS GIVES HIS PARABLE OF THE PRODIGAL SON (LUKE 15:11-32).

In His third and most extensive parable about the lost being found, Jesus describes a lost son. A man had two sons. One day the younger son asked his father to give him his share of the inheritance. So, the father divided his possessions between his two sons. The younger son became prodigal with his possessions. He went off to a distant land, squandered his wealth, and found himself destitute. He sunk so low that he ended up feeding pigs and living off their food. No one would help him. Eventually this wayward son came to his senses. He decided to return home, seek his father's forgiveness, and work as one of his father's hired hands.

What the prodigal son didn't realize was that his father still loved him. In spite of the son's failures, the father was ready to receive him back as a member of the family. In fact, the father was waiting and watching for his son's return. When he saw his son approaching, the father ran to him and lovingly embraced him. He called his servants and instructed them to clothe his son in the finest robe, jewelry, and shoes. He ordered that a fattened calf be prepared for a feast celebrating the return of his son. The father told his servants that his son had been dead and was alive again. He was lost but was now found.

However, Jesus' parable of the prodigal son didn't stop here. Jesus went on to describe the attitude of the older brother. The wayward son's brother had remained faithful to the family and the farm. When he learned that his erring brother had returned home, instead of rejoicing he became jealous. The faithful son refused to join in on the celebration. The boys' father went to his older son and listened to his complaint. The older son protested. He reminded his father that he had been faithful in every way and accused his father of never throwing a banquet in his honor. The father assured his older son that his faithfulness had not been overlooked. The entire estate belonged to this older son. But the older son should not withhold love and forgiveness from his erring brother. Instead, he should join in on the celebration. After all, the prodigal son had been dead and was now alive. He was lost, but was now found.

Jesus' parables remind us that we are all lost in sin and in need of God's forgiveness. They also teach us that God, our heavenly Father, eagerly desires our return. Once we've turned back to God through faith in Jesus Christ, we should eagerly participate in the joy of seeing others who are lost experience God's forgiveness and restored fellowship with Him.

9

THE LATER JUDEAN AND
PEREAN MINISTRY OF JESUS
(PART 3)

HAVING LEFT JERUSALEM AND CROSSED OVER THE Jordan River into Perea, Jesus continued to proclaim the good news of God's kingdom. However, Jesus also knew that His time was short. It would be only a matter of weeks before Passover would arrive, the Passover during which Jesus would give His life for our sins.

Jesus' Ministry in and around Perea (Continued)

During Jesus' time in Perea, He had again found it necessary to defend His practice of healing people on the Sabbath day. He also challenged those who wanted to be His followers to count the cost of discipleship. In addition, Jesus had emphasized God's love for lost sinners. Before returning across the Jordan River to the region of Judea, Jesus would present two more parables and instruct His followers about the nature of being a true servant.

₱137—Jesus Gives His Parable of the Shrewd Manager (Luke 16:1-18).

One of Jesus' more puzzling parables involved a shrewd household manager. Jesus told His disciples that a rich man accused his household manager of mismanaging his wealth. The rich man instructed his manager to prepare a report before being discharged from his responsibilities. This shrewd manager went to the rich man's debtors and struck a bargain. If these debtors would make a partial payment of their debts, the manager would write off the rest of their debts and clear their accounts. When the rich man discovered what his dishonest manager had done he, though having been cheated out of a great deal of wealth, commended the manager for his shrewd business dealings.

Jesus used this unusual parable to emphasize a point. Even the dishonest people of this world show more practical prudence than many of God's people. Jesus certainly wasn't encouraging His disciples to act dishonestly. He did, however, challenge them to be shrewd in their dealings with unbelievers. Jesus told them to use whatever worldly wealth they might have to influence people for their eternal good. This use of wealth would doubtless include acts of benevolence that could help needy people see the love of God. It might also include acts of hospitality toward the rich that would contribute to building trusted relationships and thereby lay a foundation for sharing the gospel.

Jesus went on to say that those who can be trusted with little will be entrusted with more, while those who are dishonest with little will be dishonest with more. We're to prove our trustworthiness in little things so that God will entrust us with greater things. We must be faithful with whatever worldly wealth we have in order for God to entrust us with true, spiritual riches. In other words, Jesus encourages us to be honest in all our dealings. Honesty in earthly matters will prove our worth when it comes to spiritual responsibilities. However, Jesus also warned His disciples not to become trapped by worldly wealth. We can't serve two masters. We can't serve God and money at the same time. We must make money our servant rather than being servants to our money. God alone must be our master.

Some of the greedy Pharisees who heard Jesus talking about money in this way mocked His teachings. Jesus accused these Pharisees of valuing that which is detestable in God's sight. They valued money, while God values character. They valued power, while God values the good news of salvation. Jesus declared that the Scriptures would be fulfilled—not even the least stroke of the pen would fail to be accomplished. These Scriptures warned of ignoring or abusing the law. For example, Jesus referred briefly to the subject of divorce. He said that a man who divorces his wife and marries another woman commits adultery. God's Word must be honored in every aspect of life, including marriage and our use of money.

#138—Jesus Gives His Parable of the Rich Man and Lazarus (Luke 16:19-31).

Because the Pharisees, like many people, were so enamored with wealth, Jesus gave His parable of the rich man and Lazarus. So graphic is Jesus' description in this parable that some have come to view it as a real story rather than a parable. Jesus described two men, a rich man and a beggar. The rich man enjoyed all the luxuries life could offer. He dressed well and ate well every day. The beggar, named Lazarus, lay at the rich man's gate covered with sores. He lived off the scraps of food that were discarded from the rich man's table. So destitute was this poor beggar that dogs would come and lick his sores. Jesus couldn't have painted a greater contrast between two men.

Jesus continued His story, saying that both the rich man and the beggar died. The beggar was carried by angels to Abraham's side, a phrase portraying heaven. The rich man, however, found himself in the torments of hell. From hell he looked up and saw Lazarus enjoying the bliss of heaven. So the rich man called to Abraham, asking him to send Lazarus to bring just a drop of water to ease his agony. Abraham pointed out that the rich man had enjoyed all the luxuries of the first life, while Lazarus was now enjoying the blessings of eternal life. Furthermore, Abraham pointed out, there is a great chasm between heaven and hell preventing an interchange between these two infinitely different places.

The rich man then begged Abraham to send Lazarus back to earth in order to warn his brothers about the horrors of hell. Abraham simply said that the Scriptures were clear and readily available to the rich man's brothers. The rich man pressed his request. He said that if someone like Lazarus returned from the dead his message would carry more weight than the Scriptures and would prompt an attitude of repentance. Abraham assured the rich man that if people wouldn't believe the Scriptures, they wouldn't be convinced even if someone rose from the dead.

The story of the rich man and Lazarus points to the literal existence of heaven and hell, the need for repentance in this lifetime, and the power of the Word of God. It also teaches us that some people will reject God's truth even in the face of a great miracle, including the miracle of Jesus' resurrection.

139—JESUS TEACHES ABOUT SERVICE (LUKE 17:1-10).

While Jesus took time to teach the crowds, He never neglected His disciples. Often He would give them special instructions, either building on their immediate encounters and experiences or offering new insights on new topics. On one of these occasions, Jesus taught His disciples about personal sin, repentance, forgiveness, faith, and service.

Jesus first warned His disciples about the danger of causing others to fall into sin. Whether by example or instruction, we must never become a stumbling stone to someone else's faith. Jesus said that those who cause others, particularly the "little ones" or novice believers, to stumble will be subject to severe judgment. It would be better, Jesus declared, for a person to be thrown into the sea with a millstone tied around his or her neck, that is, to experience a premature physical death, than to lead others away from their faith in Jesus Christ.

Jesus then told His disciples that it is appropriate and necessary for us to rebuke a sinning brother in order to bring about that fellow believer's restoration. If the sinning brother or sister repents, we're to extend forgiveness. Even if someone sins against us seven times in one day and each time repents we're to keep on forgiving him or her. Our forgiveness should know no limits.

At this point the apostles asked Jesus to increase their faith. It's noteworthy that these twelve men who had followed Jesus so closely were able to recognize their lack of faith and their need for further growth. Jesus assured His disciples that even if their faith was as small as a tiny mustard seed they could command a mulberry tree to be uprooted and planted in the sea. While our faith should be growing, it's the object of our faith more than the amount of our faith that matters most. Jesus is the object of our faith, and all things are possible through Him.

Jesus then concluded this private lesson with His disciples by describing what it means to be a servant. A servant doesn't expect his master to serve him. Instead, even after a long day of hard work a servant expects to continue laboring for his master until every need is satisfied. The servant works hard, eats last, and expects no gratitude for simply performing his duty. As servants of Jesus Christ we're to obey His will, while recognizing our own unworthy status. Our worth is found only in our relationship with our Master, Jesus Christ. Jesus wasn't implying that He would be ungrateful for our service.

In fact, we know that the Lord will reward His servants greatly. However, our service as Jesus' followers is to be characterized, not by selfish expectations, but by industry and humility.

#140—Jesus Raises Lazarus from the Dead (John 11:1-44).

While Jesus was engaged in teaching His disciples, He received word that a very close friend was sick. Lazarus and his two sisters, Mary and Martha, lived in Bethany, a town on the outskirts of Jerusalem. This faithful family had served as hosts to Jesus and His disciples on at least one previous occasion, and may have done so often during Jesus' visits to Jerusalem. Now, Lazarus had become extremely ill. Mary and Martha sent for Jesus, knowing that He alone could heal their brother. However, when Jesus received word of Lazarus' condition, He waited two full days before making His way to Bethany.

When Jesus told His disciples that they were going back to Judea they were greatly alarmed. They reminded Jesus that the Jewish leaders in Jerusalem wanted to kill Him. Jesus assured His disciples that He would not be put to death prematurely but would accomplish His mission. He then told them that Lazarus had died and that He must go spend time with Lazarus' family. One of Jesus' disciples, Thomas, expressed his willingness to go back to Jerusalem with Jesus even if it meant his own death.

When Jesus and His disciples arrived outside Bethany they discovered that Lazarus had already been dead for four days. As was the custom, Lazarus would have been buried immediately. Many people had gathered to comfort Mary and Martha in their time of loss. When Martha heard that Jesus had arrived, she went to Him and expressed her regret that Jesus hadn't been there to heal her brother. Jesus reassured Martha that Lazarus would rise again, and invited her to trust in Him as the resurrection and the life. Martha then went and told Mary that Jesus had arrived. Mary got up quickly and went out to see Jesus. Many of those who were present followed her, assuming that she was returning to Lazarus' grave. Mary, like her sister, expressed to Jesus her regret that He had not been present. She, too, believed in Jesus' healing power. Jesus was deeply moved by the deep sense of grief that these two women were experiencing, and asked to see Lazarus' grave. There at the tomb Jesus burst into tears. He certainly wept for the loss of His friend Lazarus. He wept over the suffering that Lazarus' death had brought on Mary and Martha. He probably also wept for the sinful state of all humanity that produces such suffering and death.

Having wept over Lazarus' grave, Jesus did something quite unexpected. He told the people to remove the stone that covered the mouth of the grave. Jesus then prayed to God the Father, thanking Him for the miracle that was about to occur. Finally, Jesus yelled into the tomb, "Lazarus, come out!" Still wrapped in his grave clothes, Lazarus emerged from the tomb alive. His sisters must have been elated. The crowd certainly was stunned. But no one really needed to be surprised by this display of life-giving power. After all, Jesus is the resurrection and the life.

₱141—CAIAPHAS PROPHESIES AGAINST JESUS (JOHN 11:45-53).

Jesus' miracle of raising Lazarus from the dead brought about a mixed reaction. Many who witnessed this miracle put their faith in Jesus. But some went instead to report to the Pharisees. The Pharisees and chief priests called a meeting of the Jewish ruling council known as the Sanhedrin. These religious and political leaders of Judaism were aghast at hearing about Jesus' latest miracle. They expressed their fear that if more people turned to Jesus the Roman authorities might see this movement as an open rebellion. If the Romans intervened, the Jewish leaders would lose their place of influence. At that point the High Priest, Caiaphas, spoke up. He declared that it would be better for one person—Jesus—to die than for the Jewish nation to perish. When writing his Gospel, the apostle John took this statement to mean much more than Caiaphas intended. Jesus would indeed die for His nation, not as a political pawn, but as a redeeming sacrifice for the sins of all people. It was at this meeting of the Sanhedrin that the Jewish leaders determined to put Jesus to death.

Jesus' Ministry in and around Ephraim

During the final weeks before His crucifixion, Jesus avoided Jerusalem. However, He never retreated from His opponents out of a sense of fear. Instead, knowing that He must die at just the right time and under the right circumstances, He left Jerusalem only temporarily. His time had not yet come, but it would soon arrive.

#142—JESUS WITHDRAWS TO EPHRAIM (JOHN 11:54).

Jesus was aware of the fact that the Jewish leaders had determined to put Him to death. Therefore, He led His disciples away from the heart of His opposition to the remote village of Ephraim. Ephraim was located near the Judean desert. Jesus' ministry began in the Judean desert, where He overcame Satan's temptations. It was near the Judean desert, in and around Ephraim, that Jesus would complete His public ministry. Ephraim became the staging area for Jesus' final ministry tour that took Him as far north as Galilee and as far east as Perea.

#143—JESUS HEALS TEN LEPERS (LUKE 17:11-19).

Jesus and His disciples traveled north again, along the border separating Samaria and Galilee. As He entered one of the villages of that area, Jesus encountered ten men who were suffering from the dreaded disease of leprosy. From a distance these men called to Jesus, asking for Him to pity their condition and heal them. The Old Testament instructed those who were cleansed of leprosy to show themselves to the priests in order to confirm their healing. Jesus instructed these ten lepers to go to the priests, implying that they would be healed. In fact, as these men started on their way, they were completely healed. One of these lepers, a Samaritan, returned to thank Jesus. Jesus expressed His disappointment that the other nine men whom He had healed didn't likewise return to thank Him. Only the Samaritan showed gratitude. Jesus affirmed this Samaritan's faith and sent him on his way.

#144—JESUS TEACHES ABOUT THE SECOND COMING (LUKE 17:20-37).

One day some Pharisees asked Jesus to satisfy their curiosity about the future. They wanted to know when God's kingdom would arrive. Jesus told these inquisitive Pharisees that identifying the arrival of God's kingdom wouldn't be the result of astute observation. Nor would the kingdom arrive in limited population pockets. God's worldwide kingdom, Jesus said, is "within you," or probably a better translation, "among you." The kingdom of God is to be identified with the person of Jesus Christ. He is the Messiah. He came to offer God's kingdom to God's people. However, because the people of God rejected Jesus, God's kingdom would be delayed until Jesus' second coming.

Jesus took this opportunity to instruct His disciples in more detail about the future. This brief account foreshadows Jesus' lengthier description of end time events in His Olivet Discourse a few days prior to His crucifixion. Jesus warned His disciples that He would be taken from them, but would return visibly, powerfully, and undeniably. His return will be like lightening, immediately evident to everyone. As in the days of Noah and Lot, people will be caught off guard when God intervenes in human affairs. Judgment will fall, and no one will have time to re-order their lives in that day. Those who deserve judgment will be sent away, excluded forever from God's kingdom. However, God will welcome into His kingdom those who have prepared themselves through faith in Jesus Christ.

¶145—Jesus Gives Two Parables about Prayer (Luke 18:1-14).

Jesus had modeled a life of prayer. He now presented a parable to His disciples, teaching them to be persistent in their prayers. In this parable, Jesus described an unjust judge and an unrequited widow. The widow pleaded with the judge for justice against her adversary. The judge refused to listen to the widow's pleas. However, because the widow persisted in asking the judge for justice, the judge eventually granted her request. Jesus then said that God, who is no unjust judge, will eventually establish justice on behalf of His people due to their persistent prayers. Jesus ended this parable with a puzzling question. He asked, "However, when the Son of Man comes will he find faith on the earth?" Jesus may have intended this question to spur His disciples on to deeper faith and persistent prayer.

Jesus then turned to His wider audience, which included some self-righteous individuals. He told them another parable about prayer. In this parable two men went to the temple to pray, one a Pharisee and the other a tax collector. The Pharisee prayed about how good he was, highlighting for God his self-righteous life. The tax collector, however, dared not even look up toward heaven. He beat his chest over his personal despair and begged, "God, be merciful to me, a sinner." Jesus declared that the tax collector, not the Pharisee, went away justified in God's sight. Prayer must flow from humble hearts that depend totally on God for forgiveness and acceptance.

⏸146—JESUS TEACHES ABOUT DIVORCE (MATTHEW 19:1-12; MARK 10:1-12).

Jesus' travels in the weeks prior to His crucifixion took Him again to the region east of the Jordan River. Large crowds continued to follow Him and benefit from His teaching. Some Pharisees also followed along in the crowd. One day they tested Jesus by asking whether or not a man could divorce his wife for any reason. Divorce was a topic of debate then as it is now. Jesus pointed out that Moses' law permitted divorce, but this permission was based on the hardness, or sinfulness, of the human heart. God's creation design, by contrast, intended that a husband and wife remain faithful to each other throughout their lifetime. Since God joins two people in the mysterious bonds of marriage, humans should not sever these bonds. Jesus did acknowledge that human sin, specifically the sin of adultery, breaks the marriage covenant. Nevertheless, God designed marriage to last a lifetime. Jesus' disciples then suggested to Him that it might be better not to marry at all. Jesus said that some people would be called to such a celibate lifestyle, but not everyone would find such a spiritual commitment to be an acceptable alternative to marriage. Jesus endorsed both marriage and a single lifestyle as legitimate paths for His followers. Each Christian should follow the path to which God calls us.

#147—JESUS BLESSES THE LITTLE CHILDREN (MATTHEW 19:13-15; MARK 10:13-16; LUKE 18:15-17).

One particularly fascinating insight into Jesus' nature is found in His enjoyment of children. He loved children, and children loved Him. They weren't threatened by Jesus, which shows us that Jesus must have had an extremely winsome demeanor. When parents began to bring their children to Jesus for His blessing, the disciples rebuked them. They assumed that Jesus was either too important or too busy to deal with children. But Jesus welcomed these children, stating that the kingdom of God belongs to such little ones. We must all receive God's kingdom as little children, without pretense or pride, but humbly and innocently trusting in Jesus. Jesus then took these children in His arms and blessed them. Did He spend a few moments talking with them or playing with them as well? This would certainly fit the tender character of our loving Lord.

#148—JESUS MEETS A RICH YOUNG RULER (MATTHEW 19:16-30; MARK 10:17-31; LUKE 18:18-30).

Along the way, a rich young ruler ran up to Jesus and asked what requirements he must meet in order to inherit eternal life. Jesus recited several of the commandments and said that if this young man obeyed the commandments he would have eternal life. The rich young ruler claimed to have obeyed these commandments perfectly from his boyhood. Jesus then instructed the man to sell his riches, give his money to the poor, and follow Him. But the rich young ruler wasn't as perfect as he imagined himself to be.

He may have lived a moral life, but he still harbored greed and covetousness in his heart. When Jesus instructed him to give away his wealth, the man went away very sad. He had no intention of relinquishing his wealthy lifestyle in order to follow Jesus.

Jesus then told His disciples that wealth is often a hindrance to faith. He expressed this idea by saying that it was easier for a camel to go through the eye of a sewing needle than for a rich man to enter God's kingdom. The disciples then asked who, after all, could be saved. If God's blessing wasn't measured by wealth, how could anyone be sure of his or her acceptance by God? Jesus told His disciples that salvation comes from God, not from human effort. No one can perfectly obey God's holy commandments. Therefore, God must provide another way. Nothing is impossible with God, and God has provided salvation through His Son, Jesus Christ.

Peter, still puzzling over Jesus' teachings about wealth, pointed out that he and the other disciples had left everything to follow Jesus. Jesus assured Peter that God will abundantly reward, both in this life and in eternity, everyone who makes sacrifices for Him.

149—JESUS TEACHES ABOUT GRACE (MATTHEW 20:1-16).

In an unusually challenging parable, Jesus described the nature of God's abundant grace. He described a landowner who went out early one morning to hire men to work in his vineyard. The landowner promised to pay each worker a full day's wage, one denarius. Throughout the day the landowner found more men and employed them in his vineyard. Some men worked only half a day, and some only one hour at the end of the day. When the day was over, the landowner paid those who had worked only an hour or only part of the day a full day's pay, one denarius. Those who had worked all day expected a greater reward, but soon discovered that they, too, were paid one denarius. These workers complained to the landowner about this seeming inequity. But the landowner pointed out that these men agreed to their wages at the beginning of the day. Rather than complain about their remuneration they should rejoice that the other workers had benefited so well. Instead of looking at themselves, they should look at others. In God's kingdom, Jesus said, the last will be first and the first will be last. God will grant His grace equally to all who turn to Christ by faith, whether they do so early in their lives or in the last hour.

#150—JESUS TEACHES ABOUT HIS DEATH AND ABOUT SERVANTHOOD (MATTHEW 20:17-28; MARK 10:32-45; LUKE 18:31-34).

Jesus was now making His way back to Jerusalem. He again took His disciples aside and warned them that in Jerusalem He would be betrayed to the religious authorities, condemned, and crucified. But He assured His disciples that He would rise from the dead on the third day. The disciples still couldn't grasp what Jesus meant by these warnings. Their minds must have been absorbed in thoughts about the kingdom of God rather than Jesus' mission. This preoccupation with the kingdom is evident in what happened next.

James and John had been pondering their position in God's kingdom. Their mother, who was well known to Jesus, went with her two sons to ask Him to grant a special favor. They requested Jesus' assurance that James and John would have the honored positions in God's kingdom. They wanted to sit at Jesus' left and right hand. Had they not yet learned that Jesus honored humility? Jesus asked these two daring disciples whether or not they could drink the cup that He would soon have to drink. They boldly assured Jesus that they were up for the task. Jesus said that James and John would indeed drink a cup of suffering. However, granting positions in God's kingdom was the prerogative of the Father. Jesus could not grant their request.

Understandably, when the other disciples learned about James' and John's request they were indignant. Who did these two brothers think they were? Jesus gathered His twelve disciples together and reminded them that the Gentile rulers were obsessed with issues of power and authority. In contrast, Jesus' followers must be committed to servanthood. The greatest among Jesus' followers is the one who serves. After all, Jesus didn't come to be served but to serve others. He came to give His life as a ransom for lost people. Jesus must have been disappointed that, while He had been warning about His impending death, His disciples were posturing themselves for greatness.

#151—JESUS HEALS TWO BLIND MEN AT JERICHO (MATTHEW 20:29-34; MARK 10:46-52; LUKE 18:35-43).

Jesus and His disciples had now returned to the west side of the Jordan River, to the town of Jericho. There,

Jesus encountered two blind men. Matthew's Gospel alone mentions that there were two men, Mark's alone identifies one of the men as having the name Bartimaeus, and Luke's alone states that this encounter occurred when Jesus was entering rather than leaving Jericho. These discrepancies have caused some people to suspect that the Bible is inaccurate. However, it may well be that one blind man by the name of Bartimaeus was present in the crowd when Jesus entered Jericho and, together with a blind friend, actually approached Jesus when He was leaving Jericho.

A large crowd was constantly surrounding Jesus. Blind Bartimaeus and his friend called to Jesus through the crowd, identifying Him as the Son of David and begging for His mercy. The crowd tried to silence these two blind men, but they persisted in their plea. Jesus stopped, called the men to Him, and asked what they wanted. "We want to see," they told Jesus. Jesus immediately granted their request. Instantly they could see! They followed Jesus, praising God, as did the rest of the crowd.

#152—JESUS MEETS ZACCHAEUS (LUKE 19:1-27).

When Jesus was entering Jericho, a man by the name of Zacchaeus wanted to see Him. Zacchaeus was a wealthy tax collector, but was too short to see over the crowd. Apparently no one made room for him to get through, since he was a despised tax collector. So Zacchaeus ran ahead of the crowd and climbed up into a sycamore fig tree in order to get a glimpse of Jesus as He passed by. When Jesus arrived at that very spot He stopped, looked up at Zacchaeus, and invited Himself to

Zacchaeus' home. Zacchaeus was elated. However, many of the people took offense at Jesus for being the guest of such a sinner. Transformed by Jesus' acceptance and love, Zacchaeus told Jesus that he would give half of his wealth to the poor and abundantly repay anyone whom he had cheated. Jesus declared that salvation had entered this man's house that day. Even though Zacchaeus was a tax collector, a dishonest and sinful man by human standards, Jesus had come to seek and save the lost. Zacchaeus was no longer lost. He had encountered Jesus, and Jesus had changed his life.

Because He was approaching Jerusalem and because some of the people thought that He would institute God's kingdom immediately, Jesus told a parable about waiting. A certain nobleman was going away to a distant country to be appointed as king. The nobleman appointed ten of his servants to oversee his estate, each servant receiving ten minas, equal measures of money, to use in his absence. When the nobleman returned he discovered that some of his servants had invested his money wisely, earning him even greater wealth. But one servant hid the money away until the nobleman returned. The nobleman rewarded the faithful servants and granted them greater responsibilities in his kingdom. However, the fearful, unfaithful servant received only the reprimand of his master. He had no reward in the nobleman's kingdom. Finally, the nobleman put his enemies, those who opposed his royal appointment, to death. Jesus was warning His listeners that there would be a period of waiting before He would return to establish His kingdom. His followers should serve Him faithfully. Those who were faithful would be given greater responsibilities in His kingdom, while the fearful would have no reward. Furthermore, those who opposed Jesus would be judged at His return. We must be faithful in our service to Christ while we await His return and the future kingdom of God.

10

THE DEATH AND RESURRECTION OF JESUS (PART 1)

DURING HIS NEARLY THREE AND A HALF YEARS OF public ministry, Jesus had healed countless sick people, cast out numerous demons, and taught multitudes the good news about God's coming kingdom. He had also raised up a cadre of disciples. At the same time, Jesus experienced rejection in His home town, rejection by His family, and rejection by the religious leaders. So great was this rejection that Jesus' life was in danger through much of the later phase of His ministry. No place was His life more at risk than in Jerusalem, the center of Judaism. Now the time had come for Jesus to return to Jerusalem. He would do so without hesitation, knowing full well that the time for His death had arrived. Only through His sacrificial death could Jesus fulfill His earthly mission of redeeming lost sinners.

The Passion Week

The days leading up to Jesus' crucifixion are known as the Passion Week. The "passion" of Jesus Christ refers to His suffering. During that week that would culminate in the cross and the empty tomb, Jesus presented Himself as Israel's king, engaged in open debate with His opponents, taught His disciples, and surrendered Himself to the Father's will. The four Gospels devote a great deal of space to this week, indicating that what took place during the Passion Week was monumental in human history.

153—JESUS ARRIVES AT BETHANY (JOHN 11:55—12:1).

It was spring time, time for the Jewish Feast of Passover. People from all over the countryside made their way to Jerusalem for the feast. Many wondered if Jesus would attend the feast, knowing that tensions ran high between Him and the religious leaders. In fact, these leaders had given instructions that the people should report Jesus' arrival so that they could arrest Him. Six days before the Passover Jesus did arrive. He went to the outlying town of Bethany to stay with Lazarus, whom He had recently raised from the dead. Whether or not anyone reported Jesus' arrival to the Pharisees we do not know. Jesus, however, would soon make His presence impossible to miss.

#154—Jesus is Anointed by Mary (Matthew 26:6-13; Mark 14:3-9; John 12:2-11).

While Jesus was in Bethany, some of His friends held a dinner in His honor. Mary, Martha, and Lazarus were among those present. Martha, as usual, was busy serving the guests. Mary, on the other hand, took this opportunity to offer a special act of worship to Jesus. She took a very expensive jar of perfume and, while Jesus was reclining at the dinner table, poured the perfume on His feet. She then washed Jesus' feet with the perfume and dried His feet with her hair. This was an act of extravagant worship that flowed from a lovely and loving heart.

This act of worship caught everyone's attention, but one disciple in particular spoke up. Judas Iscariot complained that Mary had wasted this expensive perfume. Shouldn't she rather have sold the perfume and given the money to the poor? Judas had quickly calculated that the perfume was worth a whole year's wages. Judas' objection makes sense to our frugal minds, but fails to grasp the greatness of our Savior. Jesus deserves our best, and so much more! Judas didn't really know Jesus, and he wasn't really concerned about the poor. The disciples later learned that Judas, who was their treasurer, stole from the gifts people had given to Jesus and His disciples. Mary's act of extravagant worship was more than Judas could bear.

Jesus reprimanded Judas for dampening the spirit of this highly moving moment of worship. He said that Mary had actually used this perfume to prepare for His burial. Jesus assured Judas and the rest of His disciples that they would always have poor people who would need their help. But they wouldn't always have Jesus in their midst. He affirmed Mary's act of worship, while affirming our ongoing responsibility to help the poor.

News quickly spread that Jesus was in Bethany. Many curious Jews went to see Him and to see Lazarus as well. Reports of Lazarus' return from the dead had reverberated throughout the community. Therefore, the chief priests intended to kill not only Jesus but Lazarus too. After all, because of Lazarus many people were putting their faith in Jesus. Not only was Jesus' life at risk, but so were the lives of those who were associated with His miraculous work.

#155—JESUS' TRIUMPHAL ENTRY INTO JERUSALEM (MATTHEW 21:1-11; MARK 11:1-11; LUKE 19:28-40; JOHN 12:12-19).

The time had come for Jesus to present Himself as Israel's long awaited king. It must have been a glorious day! Jesus led His disciples the short distance from Bethany to the Mount of Olives overlooking the city of Jerusalem. He then sent two of His disciples ahead, instructing them that they would find a donkey and its colt tied nearby. They were to bring the animals to Jesus. Should their owner ask, the disciples were to simply state that the Lord needed these animals. Sure enough, the owner eagerly loaned these beasts of burden for what would become a historic event. Jesus took His place on the back of the unbroken colt and proceeded down the road to Jerusalem. This humble entrance was that of a peaceful king coming to claim His throne, just as the Old Testament predicted. As Jesus rode along, the growing crowd began to place their outer garments and palm branches on the road in front of Jesus. They shouted in the language of the Old Testament writers, "Hosanna," that is, "Save us!" The people also shouted praises and blessings to Jesus, calling Him the King of Israel. Jerusalem's great day had come. Israel's long awaited king had arrived.

Of course, the religious leaders were enraged. How dare Jesus enter Jerusalem so boldly and accept such accolades from the people! Some of the Pharisees in the crowd demanded that Jesus rebuke His disciples for their outburst of praise. Jesus replied that if His followers didn't shout His praises, then the very stones would cry out in worship. The Pharisees conferred among themselves, admitting that all their efforts to restrain the people from following Jesus were getting them nowhere. It seemed to them that the whole world had turned its eyes and hearts toward Jesus. Would that this had been so, in that day or today! Jesus had entered Jerusalem triumphantly. In just a few days Jesus would triumphantly rise from the dead. But there was still much work to do.

After entering Jerusalem in triumph, Jesus would go directly to the Temple. There He would simply look around, as if scoping out the scene of His final days. Then, since the day was drawing to a close, Jesus would leave Jerusalem and return to Bethany.

#156—JESUS WEEPS OVER JERUSALEM (LUKE 19:41-44).

As Jesus prepared to enter Jerusalem He wept. He knew that this momentary display of support and praise during His triumphal entry would all too quickly evaporate into slander and rejection. Jesus predicted that Jerusalem would one day be besieged by an enemy army, its inhabitants—young and old—violently killed, and its wall torn down. This judgment would fall on Jerusalem because she refused to recognize God's work as revealed in the person of Jesus Christ.

#157—Jesus Curses the Fig Tree (Matthew 21:18-19; Mark 11:12-14).

The day after His triumphal entry into Jerusalem, Jesus and His disciples returned to the city from their lodging in Bethany. Jesus was hungry, and saw a fig tree in the distance. Its leaves were luxuriant, hinting that the tree should have been rich with fruit. But when Jesus got closer to the fig tree He discovered that it had no figs. As if it were an object lesson of Israel's spiritually barren condition, Jesus pronounced a curse on the fruitless fig tree.

#158—Jesus Again Cleanses the Temple (Matthew 21:12-13; Mark 11:15-19; Luke 19:45-46).

Arriving back at the Temple, Jesus began to cleanse it of its unwelcome occupants. As He had done at the beginning of His public ministry, Jesus again drove away the merchants and moneychangers who had apparently reestablished their sacrilegious practices. The Temple, Jesus said, should be a house of prayer rather than a den of thieves. Jesus' bold confrontation in the Temple further antagonized the religious leaders, who began more earnestly to look for a way to put Him to death.

¶159—JESUS TEACHES, HEALS, AND RECEIVES PRAISE AT THE TEMPLE (MATTHEW 21:14-17; LUKE 19:47-48).

Every day of the Passion Week, Jesus taught in the Temple courts. He didn't fear the religious leaders in spite of their threats. Many people listened to His teachings and sought His healing touch. Jesus healed many, including those who were blind or lame. Some people continued their praise, shouting "Hosanna to the Son of David" within the Temple area. The religious leaders, unable to prevent Jesus' growing popularity, demanded that Jesus deter the people from their enthusiastic support. Jesus simply reminded His opponents what the Scriptures taught. Such praise offered by such needy "children" was ordained of God. At the end of the day, Jesus returned to Bethany for the night.

¶160—THE DISCIPLES TAKE NOTE OF THE WITHERED FIG TREE (MATTHEW 21:20-22; MARK 11:20-26).

The next day Jesus and His disciples returned to Jerusalem. Along the way the disciples noticed that the fig tree that Jesus had cursed the day before had withered from its roots. Peter pointed this out to Jesus. He and the other disciples were amazed that the tree had withered and died so quickly. Jesus assured His disciples that if they had faith and did not doubt, they could accomplish this and even greater miracles. They could command a mountain to be cast into the sea and it would obey in response to their prayers offered in faith. However, their prayers should be filled with forgiveness toward others, not just focused on displays of power.

#161—THE JEWS QUESTION JESUS' AUTHORITY (MATTHEW 21:23-27; MARK 11:27-33; LUKE 20:1-8).

The Jewish leaders in Jerusalem—the chief priests, the elders, and the teachers of the law—were looking for any possible reason to accuse and arrest Jesus. While Jesus was teaching in the Temple courts, these religious leaders demanded to know by what authority He was carrying on His work. Jesus replied by asking these pompous leaders a question of His own. Could they state by what authority John the Baptist carried out his ministry? By implication, Jesus was stating that John's authority, like His own, came from God on high. The religious leaders quickly discussed Jesus' question among themselves. If they stated that John's authority came from heaven, Jesus would have just cause for accusing them of rejecting John. However, they were afraid to say that John had no divine authority since the people considered him to be a prophet of God. Jesus had effectively backed them into a corner. They told Jesus that they couldn't tell by what authority John had preached and baptized. Jesus then stated that He saw no reason to defend His own authority before these spiritually resistant men.

#162—JESUS GIVES HIS PARABLE OF THE TWO SONS (MATTHEW 21:28-32).

Jesus then used a parable to highlight the spiritual bankruptcy of His opponents. A man had two sons whom he instructed to go to work in the vineyard. The first son refused to go, but eventually had a change of heart and obeyed his father. The second respectfully agreed to go to work in the vineyard, but never followed through. Jesus then asked which of the two sons actually obeyed his father. The answer was obvious. The son who at first rejected his father's wishes, not the son who put up a good front, was the one who was obedient. Jesus now turned His sights on His opponents. He told them that the tax collectors and sinners would enter the kingdom before these hypocritical leaders would ever get in. After all, tax collectors, prostitutes, and all kinds of sinners had responded to John's preaching, but these religious leaders refused to repent.

#163—JESUS GIVES HIS PARABLE OF THE UNPAID VINEYARD OWNER (MATTHEW 21:33-46; MARK 12:1-12; LUKE 20:9-19).

Jesus presented another parable, this one even more accusatory toward His opponents. He described a land owner who carefully prepared a vineyard and then rented it out to various tenant farmers. The man then went away on a journey. When it came time to harvest the grapes, the vineyard owner sent his servants to collect his share of the fruit. The tenant farmers, however, beat some of these servants and even killed others. The vineyard owner then decided to send his own son, thinking, "They will respect my beloved son." But the tenant farmers conspired together and killed the man's son, thinking that thereby they could lay claim to the vineyard themselves. When the vineyard owner learned what had happened to his son, he went back and executed the murderous tenant farmers and rented his vineyard to other farmers who would act responsibly and respectfully.

Jesus then said to the religious leaders who had questioned His authority that the kingdom of God would be taken from them and given to others. They were the murderous farmers in the parable. They had rejected and stoned to death the various prophets whom God had sent in the past. Now they were conspiring to kill God's beloved Son. Jesus referred to Himself as a rejected stone that the builders would eventually discover to be essential to the construction of their building. This stone would crush its opponents in righteous judgment. Rather than repenting at Jesus' warning, the chief priests and Pharisees were now more determined than ever to arrest Jesus. But they feared the crowd, and so determined to wait for a more opportune time.

#164—JESUS GIVES HIS PARABLE OF THE WEDDING BANQUET (MATTHEW 22:1-14).

Jesus presented a third parable in which He warned the religious leaders that they would be excluded from God's kingdom. In this parable Jesus described a king who prepared a wedding banquet for his son. The king sent his servants to bring the invited guests to the banquet, but those who had been invited refused to participate. The king then sent more servants, but the people ignored the invitation and went about their business. In fact, some of those who had been invited to the banquet went so far as to beat and even kill some of the king's servants. The king was rightly enraged. He sent his army and destroyed these unresponsive, murderous men. He even destroyed their city. Then the king sent his servants to invite the common people of the land to the wedding banquet. These people gladly accepted the king's invitation. Apparently the king even provided the proper clothing for this elegant event.

However, when one of the guests came to the wedding banquet without the proper wedding clothing, the king sent him away. Jesus concluded this parable by saying, "Many are called, but few are chosen." The religious leaders of His day had been called to participate in God's kingdom, but they rejected God's Son. God would judge them and their city, the great city of Jerusalem. God had also called people of all walks of life to enter into His kingdom, making provision for their salvation through Jesus Christ. But no one can enter that kingdom unless he or she appropriates God's gracious provision.

#165—THE QUESTION ABOUT PAYING TAXES TO CAESAR (MATTHEW 22:15-22; MARK 12:13-17; LUKE 20:20-26).

The plot was thickening. Jesus had trapped His opponents with a question about John the Baptist's authority. Now the religious leaders plotted to trap Jesus in His own words. They sent some of their followers to barrage Jesus with a series of questions. But Jesus proved Himself sufficient to answer every question they posed.

The first question involved paying taxes to Caesar. Those who asked this question first claimed to respect Jesus' integrity and teachings, as if baiting the trap. They then asked whether it was right for the Jewish people to pay taxes to Caesar. If Jesus said that the Jews shouldn't pay taxes, the Roman government would intervene. But if Jesus said that it was right and necessary to pay taxes to Rome, He would lose popular support because the Jews despised Rome's authority. Jesus recognized the insincerity of those who posed this question, and He answered brilliantly. He asked one of them to show Him a Roman coin, a denarius. He then asked whose portrait was on the coin. The coin bore the image of Caesar. Jesus then said, "Give to Caesar the things that are Caesar's, and to God the things that are God's." No one could argue with this logic. It was necessary to pay taxes to Rome, but even more important to give our hearts to God.

#166—THE QUESTION ABOUT THE RESURRECTION (MATTHEW 22:23-33; MARK 12:18-27; LUKE 20:27-38).

The second question Jesus' opponents raised to trap Him involved the resurrection of the body. This time the Jewish sect known as the Sadducees, who denied the resurrection and other supernatural elements of faith, posed a hypothetical situation. The law stated that if a man died childless, his brother should marry the man's wife and raise up children in his brother's name. The Sadducees described a situation in which a man, one of seven brothers, died childless. The man's brother married the widow, but likewise died childless. This situation continued until all seven brothers had married the woman and each had died without a child. The Sadducees asked which brother would be married to the woman in the resurrection. Jesus responded by pointing out the Sadducees' ignorance of the Scriptures and denial of the supernatural world. He said that in the resurrection there is no marriage. Like the angels, we will not marry or be given in marriage in heaven. We can only understand from this statement that all relationships in heaven will be far purer and superior to the best relationships we've experienced on earth. Jesus then pointed out to the skeptical Sadducees that the Scriptures described God as the God of Abraham, Isaac, and Jacob. He stated that God is not a God of the dead, but of the living. The patriarchs, therefore, must still be alive in an eternal existence. The resurrection and eternal life are spiritual realities.

#167—THE QUESTION ABOUT THE GREATEST COMMANDMENT (MATTHEW 22:34-40; MARK 12:28-34).

Finally, one of the teachers of the law, favorably impressed with Jesus' responses so far, asked Him to identify the greatest commandment in God's law. Jesus appropriately identified the command to love God with our whole heart, soul, mind, and strength as the greatest commandment. God is one, and deserves our undivided devotion. We're to love God totally, with every fiber of our being. As a bonus answer, Jesus also identified the second greatest commandment. We're to love our neighbor as ourselves. Loving God and loving our neighbor, Jesus said, summarizes the entire law. The man who had raised this question about the greatest commandment expressed his delight with Jesus' answer. Jesus assured this particular teacher of the law that he was not far from the kingdom. We can only suppose that this man, after the resurrection, put his faith in Jesus. At this point the religious leaders stopped asking Jesus questions. It was apparent that they couldn't trap Him in His teachings. In fact, Jesus' insightful responses only strengthened His cause.

⚓168—JESUS RAISES THE QUESTION ABOUT DAVID'S SON (MATTHEW 22:41-46; MARK 12:35-40; LUKE 20:39-47).

Seeing that His critics were silenced, Jesus posed a question of His own. He asked the religious leaders how the promised Messiah could be the son of David and at the same time be considered David's Lord. After all, the psalms described the Messiah in both ways. The religious leaders were stumped. They had no idea how to solve this seeming contradiction. Of course, we know that Jesus was both the Son of David and David's Lord. This was possible because Jesus is both human and divine. As a man, Jesus is a descendant of David. But as God in the flesh, Jesus is David's Lord and Savior. The religious leaders refused to acknowledge the deity of Jesus Christ and therefore couldn't answer Jesus' question.

Jesus took this opportunity to warn the crowd about the hypocrisy of the religious elite of His day. These men, Jesus said, loved to draw attention to themselves by wearing impressive robes. They loved to be greeted with honor in the marketplaces. They took the seats of honor in the synagogues and at banquets. Yet these same men, though making long prayers, would devour the necessary subsistence of a poor widow. Jesus warned that such hypocrites will be punished severely.

⚓169—JESUS DENOUNCES THE PHARISEES (MATTHEW 23:1-36).

Jesus went on to denounce the Pharisees and the teachers of the law in the harshest of terms. Matthew's

Gospel records this extended warning about hypocrisy. Jesus accused the Pharisees and the teachers of the law of misusing their spiritual authority. They loaded people with burdens but were unwilling to help carry those burdens. They dressed in such a way as to draw attention to themselves and to their supposed spirituality. They sought places of honor in the public arena. All of these pompous displays of piety fell far short of Jesus' principle that the greatest among us must be a servant to others. God humbles the proud and exalts the humble.

Jesus then went on to pronounce seven "woes," or accusations worthy of judgment, against the Pharisees and the teachers of the law. These hypocrites were guilty of shutting people out of the kingdom of heaven, enslaving converts in spiritual bondage, elevating external things over true worship, giving a tenth of their tiniest resources while neglecting justice and mercy, disregarding the inner matters of the heart, focusing on outward appearances, and persecuting God's prophets. These were weighty charges against a group of men whom most people respected for their religious zeal. But their zeal was misdirected. They were zealous for themselves and not for God.

For these reasons Jesus described the Pharisees as a brood of vipers who were condemned to spend eternity in hell. God had sent them countless prophets to warn of His judgment, but they consistently rejected God's message and His messengers. Therefore, they remained in their guilt.

#170—JESUS EXPRESSES SORROW OVER JERUSALEM (MATTHEW 23:37-39).

When Jesus concluded His verbal assault on the hypocritical religious leaders, He spoke more broadly about the judgment that would soon fall on the city of Jerusalem. This city, the center of God's work in ancient times, had over and over again rejected and killed God's messengers. Jesus longed to gather the inhabitants of Jerusalem under His protective arm just as a hen protects her chicks. But the city, its leaders, and its people refused to believe in Him. Jesus declared that Jerusalem was spiritually desolate. He would no longer make Himself available to help this city and its people until His second coming. At that time Jerusalem will welcome Jesus as its Messiah.

#171—JESUS RESPONDS TO A QUESTION BY SOME GREEK WORSHIPERS (JOHN 12:20-36).

At some point during the week leading up to Jesus' death, certain Greeks who had traveled to Jerusalem to celebrate the Feast of Passover approached Philip, one of Jesus' disciples. They sought an audience with Jesus. Philip went first to Andrew, and together they told Jesus about this request. John's Gospel gives no indication that Jesus honored this request. Jesus simply declared that His hour had finally arrived. It was time for Him to be glorified. Like a kernel of wheat that is buried and then produces many seeds, Jesus must die in order to provide salvation for all who would believe. Jesus stated that His heart was troubled. Yet He did not shirk His mission. Rather, Jesus expressed His desire to fulfill His purpose in coming into this world and prayed that the Father's name would be glorified in the process.

At that moment God the Father spoke audibly from heaven, declaring that He had indeed glorified His name and would continue to do so through the obedient work of His Son. The crowd heard God's voice indistinctly, thinking it was thunder or possibly the voice of an angel. But Jesus heard the Father's voice distinctly. He knew that His mission would be accomplished. He would be lifted up on a cross, but in so doing would draw all people to Himself. He would become the Savior of the world, offering forgiveness to all who believe. Jesus warned the crowd to put their trust in Him as the true spiritual light before it was too late.

#172—THE DISBELIEF OF THE PEOPLE (JOHN 12:37-43).

Jesus' ministry continued to divide people. In spite of His miracles many of the people refused to believe in Him. John's Gospel points out that the prophet Isaiah had predicted such unbelief. But there were many who did put their faith in Jesus as the Messiah. Even some of the religious leaders believed in Jesus. They were simply afraid to declare their faith because the Pharisees had threatened to expel from the synagogue anyone who followed Jesus. Even though some of these religious leaders believed in Jesus, they valued human recognition over God's approval.

#173—Jesus Declares His Role as a Light in the World (John 12:44-50).

At this point Jesus shouted out that anyone who believed in Him believed also in God the Father who had sent Him. Everyone who saw Jesus saw God! Jesus was the light, showing people the way out of darkness. He came to save the world, not to judge it. Judgment would come at a future day. Those who rejected Jesus would face judgment. But Jesus offered eternal life to all who would follow Him.

#174—Jesus Takes Note of the Widow's Mites (Mark 12:41-44; Luke 21:1-4).

That which has been described as Jesus' "busy day" at the Temple ended with His sweet recognition of an act of true worship. Jesus was sitting near the place where people contributed their offerings to God. Many of the rich people put generous gifts into the Temple treasury. But then along came a poor widow. She placed two tiny copper coins—two mites—into the offering. This small amount of money was nearly worthless in most people's eyes, but it would have been of great value to this woman in her destitute condition. Her gift was truly sacrificial. Jesus gathered His disciples around Him. He told them that this poor widow had given more to God than had anyone else. After all, most people had given but a portion of their wealth, but this widow had given everything she owned. God recognizes and rewards sacrificial giving.

₽175—JESUS PRESENTS HIS OLIVET DISCOURSE (MATTHEW 24:1—25:46; MARK 13:1-37; LUKE 21:5-38).

Jesus had turned His back on Jerusalem and the Jewish leaders. As He was leaving the Temple, His disciples called His attention to the magnificence of this structure. Jesus replied that, in spite of its magnificence, this Temple would one day be destroyed. Not one stone would stand on another, so complete would its destruction be. Jesus led His disciples out of Jerusalem, through the Kidron Valley, and up the slopes of the Mount of Olives. There, seated on the Mount of Olives overlooking Jerusalem and its Temple, Jesus' disciples asked Him to explain what lay ahead. When would the Temple be destroyed? What would be the signs of Jesus' return? In a lengthy discourse, Jesus unfolded God's plan for the future.

The world must experience great hardship before Jesus returns. Bold individuals will claim to have the answers to life's problems, promoting themselves as messianic saviors. Nations will wage war with one another. The earth will experience famines and earthquakes, and other natural disasters. Religious persecution will continue and intensify, but the gospel of Jesus Christ will reach around the globe. These are some of the general characteristics of the future of the world.

Jesus taught that as the day of His return draws closer, something abominable will be ensconced in God's Temple, causing God's people to flee. Gentile armies will surround and trample Jerusalem. The world will enter a time of unparalleled tribulation. Only then will Jesus return from heaven. He will come in power and great glory. At His return, God's people will be rescued and God's enemies defeated.

Jesus underscored His teachings about the end times and His return by presenting a series of parables. He first described the signs of the end times as a budding fig tree. When the fig tree sprouts leaves, summer is near. When the signs that Jesus described begin to fall into place, His return will be near. No one knows the hour of Christ's return, so it would be foolhardy to set dates. But it is appropriate to look for the signs of Jesus' second coming. Even more, it is necessary for Jesus' followers to be diligently serving Him until He returns.

Jesus then told a parable about ten virgins. These virgins went out to meet the bridegroom so that they could attend him at his marriage banquet. Each took an oil lamp, but only five of the virgins took a supply of oil for their lamps. Because the bridegroom didn't arrive as promptly as they had hoped, five of the virgins ran out of lamp oil. They had to return to town to buy more, and while they were gone they missed the arrival of the bridegroom. Jesus warned His disciples to remain watchful and be prepared at all times for His return.

Next, Jesus told a parable about a man who went away on a long journey. This man entrusted his property to his servants, giving each a different amount of money to manage in his absence. The first two servants doubled their master's wealth while he was gone, but the third servant foolishly hid the money, failing to invest it for his master. When the master returned, he rewarded the first two servants for their faithfulness. However, the master reprimanded the third servant for his lethargy and sent him away. We are to faithfully serve Jesus Christ until He returns.

Jesus concluded His Olivet Discourse by describing future judgment. When Jesus returns He will separate believers from unbelievers as a shepherd would separate sheep from goats. He will welcome believers into His kingdom, granting them eternal life. Unbelievers, however, will be sent away to eternal punishment. The stakes could not be higher. What we do with Jesus Christ in this life will determine our destiny in the next life. Jesus is the light of the world. He offers each of us eternal life. We must simply and humbly put our faith in Him.

11

THE DEATH AND RESURRECTION OF JESUS (PART 2)

JESUS HAD BOLDLY PRESENTED HIMSELF AS ISRAEL'S promised king. He had publicly confronted the Jewish leaders, proving Himself more than equal to the task of answering their questions and exposing their hypocrisy. Since the official leaders of the Jewish people had blatantly rejected Jesus, He left the Temple, never to grace its corridors again until His second coming. His life could now be measured in hours. The Passion Week was quickly coming to a dramatic conclusion. It would end with Jesus' crucifixion. But the crucifixion wouldn't be the end of the story.

The Passion Week (Continued)

The Passion Week, so prominent in the records of the four Gospel writers, reminds us that Jesus came into this world on a mission. He came to offer His life as the only acceptable sacrifice for our sins. Even though Jesus had predicted His death on several occasions, His disciples were slow to comprehend the necessity and certainty of His crucifixion.

#176—JESUS PREDICTS HIS DEATH (MATTHEW 26:1-2).

In response to His disciples' request, Jesus had unfolded the divine plan for the future in His Olivet Discourse. The scriptural prophecies that had not been fulfilled in Jesus' first coming would be fulfilled in His second coming. But the cross must come before the crown. Therefore, Jesus once again reminded His disciples that the Passover was approaching and that He would be crucified.

#177—THE JEWISH LEADERS PLOT TO KILL JESUS (MATTHEW 26:3-5; MARK 14:1-2; LUKE 22:1-2).

While Jesus was teaching His disciples, His opponents were plotting His death. The religious leaders gathered in the palace of the high priest, Caiaphas, to plan how they could kill Jesus. They determined that it would be unwise to put Jesus to death during the Passover, since He was so popular with the multitude of people who had come to Jerusalem for the feast. It's ironic that Jesus died during Passover, the exact time that the Jewish leaders decided to avoid. Passover was the time that God had chosen for

His Son to provide salvation for the world, and nothing could thwart God's plan.

#178—JUDAS ARRANGES TO BETRAY JESUS (MATTHEW 26:14-16; MARK 14:10-11; LUKE 22:3-6).

At some point during the Passion Week, Judas Iscariot made arrangements with the Jewish leaders to betray Jesus. He would bring accusations against Jesus that would warrant Jesus' arrest, trial, and crucifixion. Luke's Gospel informs us that, not surprisingly, Satan had energized Judas to perform this inexpressibly evil act. Judas' offer was just what the Jewish leaders needed to proceed with their evil plot. They gave Judas thirty pieces of silver in exchange for his role in betraying Jesus. From that point on, Judas began to look for the right opportunity to turn Jesus over to the authorities.

The Last Supper

On the night before His crucifixion Jesus gathered His disciples for a final meal, the Last Supper. Scholars have debated whether or not this meal was the customary Passover feast. Possibly Jesus ate the Passover meal with His disciples and then became the sacrificial Lamb of God the next day. It's also possible that Jesus ate a meal with His disciples much like the Passover feast and then died at the very moment that the Passover lambs were being sacrificed for the Jewish feast. In either case, Jesus was the Lamb of God who died for our sins. The Last Supper reveals Jesus' character, His mission, and His future plan for His disciples.

#179—JESUS SENDS PETER AND JOHN TO PREPARE THE PASSOVER MEAL (MATTHEW 26:17-19; MARK 14:12-16; LUKE 22:7-13).

The Synoptic Gospels—Matthew, Mark, and Luke—present the Last Supper as the Passover meal. Jesus sent Peter and John into Jerusalem to make arrangements. He told them that they would meet a man who would be carrying a water jar and they were to follow him. This man would enter the house where the Last Supper would take place. Peter and John were to tell the owner of the house that the Teacher requested the use of his upstairs room for the feast, and the man would eagerly comply. In that Upper Room the two disciples were to make preparations for the Passover meal.

#180—JESUS EATS THE PASSOVER MEAL WITH HIS DISCIPLES (MATTHEW 26:20; MARK 14:17; LUKE 22:14-18).

When evening arrived, Jesus and His disciples went to the Upper Room and, as was the practice in that day, reclined at the table which Peter and John had prepared. Jesus expressed to His disciples His great desire to celebrate this particular Passover with them. This would be His last Passover until He would again share this feast in the future kingdom of God. Then Jesus handed His disciples a cup to share, reinforcing the idea that this would be His last time with them in such a setting.

#181—THE DISCIPLES HAVE A DISPUTE OVER GREATNESS (LUKE 22:24-30).

Jesus' thoughts were focused on His fellowship with His disciples and, no doubt, His impending death. However, His disciples' thoughts were still consumed with their desires for personal greatness. Jesus interrupted their senseless conversation, reminding them that Gentile authorities were concerned about physical power. Jesus' followers, however, were to concentrate on serving others. Jesus had come into the world to serve. The disciples would indeed one day sit on thrones in God's kingdom. But for now they were to be servants to one another and to a needy world.

#182—JESUS WASHES THE DISCIPLES' FEET (JOHN 13:1-20).

As if to etch His lesson on servanthood indelibly on the hearts of His disciples, Jesus demonstrated His love in a remarkably humble way. He got up from the table, wrapped a towel around His waist, poured water into a basin, and began to wash His disciples' feet. It was customary in that culture for a host to have a servant wash the feet of his guests. Jesus took the role of a servant among His disciples. One by one, Jesus poured water on His disciples' feet. One by one He wiped their feet with the towel.

When Jesus came to Peter, Peter resisted. He had apparently misunderstood Jesus' point. Jesus was his Master and shouldn't be washing his feet. But Jesus, as Peter's Master, was thereby Peter's servant. Jesus told Peter that he would understand later the importance of this object lesson. Peter continued to resist, but Jesus told him that he had to comply in order to have a part in Jesus' ministry. At that point Peter, in his usual all-or-nothing approach, asked Jesus to wash not only his feet but his hands and head as well. Jesus assured Peter that once a person was clean there was no further need for a bath. A foot washing would be sufficient. Jesus then declared that those reclining around the table were clean, that is, spiritually accepted by God. The only exception was Judas. It's fascinating to realize that Jesus, knowing full well that Judas was plotting His death, stooped to wash Judas' feet. Who could imagine a humbler act of grace?

After Jesus had washed His disciples' feet He returned to His place at the table. Jesus then asked His disciples if they understood His actions. He noted that the disciples rightly called Him their Teacher and their Lord. Since He, their Lord, had washed their feet as a common servant, they should serve one another. To refuse to serve others is to claim a greater position than our Master, Jesus Christ. Jesus assured His disciples that they would enjoy His divine blessing if they would follow His example. At this point Jesus also hinted that one among them would betray Him.

183—JESUS WARNS OF JUDAS' BETRAYAL (MATTHEW 26:21-25; MARK 14:18-21; LUKE 22:21-23; JOHN 13:21-30).

It was true. A betrayer, one of the twelve chosen disciples, reclined at the Passover meal with Jesus. After washing His disciples' feet, Jesus became visibly troubled. He stated plainly that one of the men present would soon betray Him to the authorities. Jesus expected to die on a cross. This was His mission. But Jesus warned that great judgment would fall on the one who would betray Him.

The disciples couldn't believe their ears. Who among them would betray their Master? They even wondered if their own deceitful hearts might lead them into such a despicable act. So, one by one they asked Jesus if they would have any part in His betrayal. "Surely not I, Lord?" they questioned in turn. It appears that John sat nearest Jesus. Peter motioned to John to ask Jesus to identify the betrayer. John leaned over and, probably in a whisper, asked Jesus who would betray Him. Jesus said that He would dip a piece of bread into a dish and hand it to the betrayer. He then gave the bread to Judas Iscariot. Judas put on a surprised front, saying as the others had, "Surely not I?" Jesus said, "Yes, you."

At that moment Satan entered Judas, who had already been plotting with the authorities to betray Jesus. Jesus instructed Judas to leave quickly and carry out his diabolical plan. Since this intimate conversation probably took place in lowered voices during the course of the meal, it shouldn't be surprising that most of the disciples didn't understand that Judas was the betrayer. In fact, the rest of the disciples highly trusted Judas. They had even charged him with the financial responsibilities of the group. When Judas left the table abruptly, the disciples assumed he went to purchase something more for the feast or to give alms to the poor on their behalf. John's Gospel states that when Judas left, it was night. The darkness outside bespoke the greater darkness that resided in Judas' evil heart. Judas went out to betray Jesus to the authorities. His name will be forever remembered for this devilish act of treachery.

#184—JESUS INSTITUTES THE LORD'S SUPPER (MATTHEW 26:26-30; MARK 14:22-26; LUKE 22:19-20).

At some point after Judas left the table, Jesus used the elements of the Passover meal to institute a new memorial. Just as the Passover meal looked back at Israel's miraculous redemption from Egyptian slavery, so the new meal—the Lord's Supper, or Communion—would look back at our miraculous redemption from our slavery to sin. Jesus took a piece of bread and blessed it, indicating its new and unique significance. He then broke the bread and offered it to His disciples, saying, "Take and eat. This is my body. Do this in remembrance of me." Next, Jesus took the cup, gave thanks, and offered it to His disciples. He said, "This cup is the new covenant in my blood which is poured out for you." While we're to remember Jesus regularly through the bread and cup, Jesus stated that He would no longer drink the fruit of the vine until He drinks it with His followers in God's future kingdom.

#185—JESUS TEACHES HIS DISCIPLES ABOUT LOVE (JOHN 13:31-35).

Because Judas was no longer present, Jesus could again concentrate on teaching His disciples. His lesson focused on love. Jesus said that He would soon be glorified and the Father would be glorified through Him. Jesus' death would not end in shame but in divine and everlasting glory as it would reveal the love of God. Jesus warned

His disciples that He would soon be taken from them, and they could no longer physically follow Him. But in His absence they were to follow His commands, particularly His command to love one another. Jesus described this as a new command, one with new significance. Jesus had loved His disciples. With that same love, His disciples were to love one another. Love would forever be the badge identifying Jesus' followers. "By this," Jesus declared, "will everyone know that you are my disciples, if you love one another."

#186—JESUS TEACHES ABOUT PETER'S DENIAL (MATTHEW 26:31-35; MARK 14:27-31; LUKE 22:31-38; JOHN 13:36-38).

Jesus had said that He was going away and that His disciples could not follow Him. Peter interrupted, asking where Jesus intended to go. Jesus again said that His disciples couldn't follow Him yet, but would follow Him later. He was, of course, speaking of His death. Jesus then warned His disciples that on that very night every one of them would take offense at Him. They would scatter like sheep without a shepherd. But Jesus assured His disciples that later He would meet with them again in Galilee.

Jesus warned Peter in particular that Satan would test him, sifting him like wheat. But Jesus assured Peter that He had prayed for Peter's faith to withstand this time of testing. Later, Peter would become instrumental in strengthening the other disciples. Peter objected to this warning. He declared that, regardless of what the other disciples might do, he would never take offense at Jesus. He was ready to go to prison and even die for Jesus. Jesus turned to Peter and said that, in spite of his declaration of loyalty and courage, he would deny Jesus three times before morning arrived—"before the rooster crows." Peter insisted that he would never disown Jesus. The rest of the disciples likewise declared their unflinching devotion. Time would soon reveal how weak their hearts really were in the face of danger.

Then Jesus told His disciples that they would soon face new challenges. Previously, Jesus had instructed them to take no provisions on their journeys. Now they were to take money and provisions to help them along the way. They were even to take along a sword, Jesus told them. In other words, the disciples would face danger and hardship unmatched by anything they had experienced in Jesus' presence. Jesus would be counted by many as a law breaker, and His followers would carry the same stigma. While Jesus may not have been encouraging His disciples to take up a literal sword, the disciples quickly showed Jesus that they already possessed two swords among them. Jesus simply said to them, "That is enough." He wasn't starting a political rebellion. He wasn't raising up an army. Jesus was warning His disciples that they would walk a very difficult road.

187—Jesus Presents His Upper Room Discourse (John 14:1—16:33).

One of Jesus' lengthiest recorded discourses took place in the privacy of the Upper Room during the intimate setting of the Last Supper. On that occasion, just hours before His death, Jesus provided His disciples with warnings and assurances. He would be taken from their presence, but they would experience the powerful presence of God in a new way, through the indwelling Holy Spirit.

Jesus reassured His disciples that they did not need to be troubled in their hearts. Their faith in Him and in God the Father would see them through any difficulties that lay ahead. In the Father's house are many palatial rooms where all His children will live forever. Jesus said that He was going to heaven to prepare a place for His followers. He also assured His disciples that He would come back to take His followers to be with Him in that glorious, eternal existence. Jesus then stated that His disciples knew the way to this heavenly dwelling place.

At this point Thomas spoke up. He said that they didn't even know where Jesus was going, so they couldn't possibly know the way to get there. Jesus declared, "I am the way, the truth, and the life." Only through faith in Jesus as our Savior and God can we receive eternal life and stand in the presence of God the Father.

Philip was the next to express his concern. He asked Jesus to show them the Father, stating that such a vision would be all they would ever need. Jesus said that anyone who had seen Him had seen the Father. Within the mystery of the triune God, Jesus is one with the Father and the Holy Spirit. That is why we can pray in the name of Jesus and know that the Father hears and answers our prayers. Even though Jesus would leave this world, He would send another helper, a sort of legal advocate or counselor, to be with us at all times. That counselor is none other than the Holy Spirit. Jesus promised that, after His departure, the Holy Spirit would dwell within all true believers.

The next disciple to raise a question during Jesus' Upper Room Discourse was Judas, not Judas Iscariot who had already left to betray Jesus, but another disciple by this name. Judas asked why Jesus would show Himself only to His followers and not make a grand display of His power to the whole world. Jesus replied by emphasizing the power of love. He would not force obedience, but desired rather that people would obey His teaching because of their love for Him. Jesus then assured the disciples that the Holy Spirit would help them remember everything Jesus had taught. This work of the Holy Spirit would be essential for the writing of the New Testament later on. Jesus again encouraged His disciples not to be troubled. He would freely grant them immeasurable peace.

Jesus next compared Himself to a vine. Jesus' Father is the gardener, and His disciples are the branches. We're to remain in vital relationship with Jesus, abiding in Him. Only then can we bear fruit for God. God may at times prune our lives in order to make our lives more fruitful. Abiding in Christ means to abide in His love, and we do so by living in obedience to His commands, particularly His command to love one another. After all, Jesus showed the greatest form of love by laying down His life for us. We bring joy to Jesus when we obey Him. Furthermore, Jesus considers us to be not simply servants, but close friends!

Although Jesus' followers enjoy a special relationship with God, their relationship with the world will forever be strained. Jesus warned that the world would hate His disciples because it hated Him. It would persecute

Christians because it persecuted Christ. Nonetheless, we're to continue testifying about Jesus' work in our lives. Jesus assured His disciples that the Holy Spirit would come and help them remain faithful in the face of opposition. The Spirit would convict the unbelieving world of its sinful condition while guiding Jesus' disciples into all truth.

While Jesus talked about leaving this world, the disciples around the table whispered to one another their confusion over His words. Where was Jesus going? Why wouldn't they see Him any longer? Jesus, knowing their uncertainty about His words, told them that soon they would mourn while the world would rejoice. But their grief would turn to joy. Jesus was going to die, rise again, and return to God the Father in heaven. These were difficult concepts for the disciples to grasp at the moment. Jesus ended His Upper Room Discourse by once again warning His disciples that they would soon scatter because of the events that would transpire. But Jesus also promised to grant them peace. In the world they would experience trouble, but in Him they would have peace because Jesus had overcome the world.

#188—JESUS OFFERS HIS HIGH PRIESTLY PRAYER (JOHN 17:1-26).

Jesus then entered into a prayer that reflected His unique, priestly role. Like the High Priest of ancient times, Jesus interceded for His people. This prayer, therefore, has come to be known as Jesus' High Priestly Prayer. In this prayer Jesus first prayed for Himself. He asked the Father to glorify Him again. Jesus had come to provide eternal life, and now that work was nearly completed. Jesus then prayed for His disciples. He asked that these men might experience

God's protection from the world and from the attacks of Satan. Finally, Jesus prayed for future generations of believers, those who would become His followers through the testimony of the disciples. Jesus' prayer for us is that we might live in loving unity with one another.

#189—JESUS PRAYS IN THE GARDEN OF GETHSEMANE (MATTHEW 26:36-46; MARK 14:32-42; LUKE 22:39-46; JOHN 18:1).

As the night progressed, Jesus led His disciples out of the Upper Room, across the Kidron Valley, and into an olive grove at the base of the Mount of Olives. This grove, known as the Garden of Gethsemane, became the scene of a great spiritual battle. It was there that Jesus, in His humanity, wrestled with the imminent torments of the cross. It was there that Jesus overcame the enemy.

When they had arrived at Gethsemane, Jesus told His disciples to pray. He then led Peter, James, and John a bit farther. Becoming deeply distressed, Jesus told these three disciples that His soul was overwhelmed with sorrow. He asked Peter, James, and John to keep watch with Him and to pray for strength. Then Jesus went still farther into the Garden of Gethsemane to pray privately. There He fell to the ground and asked God the Father to, if at all possible, remove the "cup" that He must soon drink. The horror of the cross—the horror of separation from the Father—was too great for Jesus, in His humanity, to bear. But Jesus affirmed His consistent devotion to the Father's will. Jesus prayed so intensely that His sweat became drops of blood, and an angel came to strengthen Him in this hour of need.

After some time, Jesus went back to His disciples only to find them sleeping instead of praying. He woke them and again urged them to pray. Then Jesus went away by Himself and repeated His prayer to God the Father, again concluding His prayer by committing Himself to the Father's will. Jesus went back to His disciples. Again they were sleeping. This time Jesus didn't wake them up, but returned for a third season of prayer. At the end of His prayer, Jesus woke up His disciples and told them that the appointed hour had come. He instructed them to get up and go meet His betrayer. The hour of darkness had arrived. Jesus would be betrayed, arrested, tried, and crucified. Through prayer, Jesus had prepared Himself for everything that lay ahead. He would lay down His life for our sins.

12

THE DEATH AND RESURRECTION OF JESUS (PART 3)

THE DARKEST DAY IN HUMAN HISTORY WAS FOLLOWED three days later by the brightest day. Jesus, the Son of God, died on a Roman cross. He was buried in a borrowed tomb. But this same Jesus rose victoriously from the grave. Tragedy and triumph, agony and victory, redemption and resurrection—all were part of the mission that Jesus Christ accomplished on our behalf. Jesus had to carry a cross before He could wear a crown. He had to pay for our sins before He could freely give us eternal life. He became our sacrifice so that He could be our Savior.

The Crucifixion

⟨190—Judas Betrays Jesus in the Garden (Matthew 26:47-49; Mark 14:43-45; Luke 22:47-48; John 18:2-3).

The Garden of Gethsemane had proven to be a spiritual battle ground in which Jesus, the Son of God and the Son of Man, had won a great victory. He had submitted Himself completely to the will of the Father and was ready to die for the sins of the world. Gethsemane also proved to be a battle ground in which Judas Iscariot forfeited his soul for all eternity. Judas had arranged to betray Jesus. Now the time had come. Judas arrived at Gethsemane along with an armed crowd sent by the chief priests and elders of the Jewish nation. In order to avoid confusion in the darkness of the hour, Judas had arranged with the mob to identify Jesus with a kiss. Such mockery! Judas would feign respect for his former Master with the normal greeting of affection, but in so doing would be handing Jesus over to the authorities for His execution. Judas approached Jesus and kissed Him. Jesus, of course, recognized this act for what it was—betrayal.

⟨191—Jesus is Arrested (Matthew 26:50-56; Mark 14:46-52; Luke 22:49-53; John 18:4-12).

After Judas betrayed Jesus, Jesus turned to those who had come to arrest Him and asked whom they sought. They replied, "Jesus of Nazareth." Jesus calmly declared, "I am!" This simple statement carried with it all the authority of God, the great I Am. These words swept over those who had come to arrest Jesus. The mob drew back and fell to the ground under the awesome power of Jesus' presence. Jesus again asked whom they sought, and the mob again answered that they were looking for Jesus. Jesus never tried to dodge their evil intentions, but simply identified Himself as the one for whom they were looking. He also told the mob to let His disciples go, since He alone was the target of their hatred.

At this point the disciples, at last aware of what was taking place so quickly around them, asked Jesus if they should resist this cruel crowd. As the men stepped forward to arrest Jesus, Peter took a sword and swung wildly in defense of his Master. He struck a servant of the High Priest, cutting off his ear. Jesus intervened immediately. He told Peter to put away his sword. After all, if Jesus wanted to escape He could call on the angels of heaven to protect Him. Then Jesus, in a remarkable show of grace, touched the man whose ear had been severed and healed him.

Jesus then addressed the mob, asking why they had come so heavily armed. After all, Jesus wasn't leading a rebellion. In addition, He had been openly teaching every day in the Temple courts and the officials had made no effort to arrest Him. But Jesus knew that the darkness of the hour revealed the darkness of these men's evil intentions. Jesus submitted Himself to be bound and taken away. At this point Jesus' disciples fled, just as He had predicted. Marks' Gospel refers to an unidentified young man who, apparently wearing only his bedclothes, followed Jesus after His arrest. The mob tried to arrest him, but he escaped their grasp. Some have suggested that this young man may have been Mark, the author of this Gospel. Jesus had been betrayed by Judas, arrested by the Jewish authorities, and abandoned by His disciples. He would now face a series of mock trials before heading to the cross.

#192—Jesus' Trial before Annas (John 18:13-14, 19-23).

The crowd that had arrested Jesus led Him first to Annas, the father-in-law of the High Priest Caiaphas and an influential individual within the Jewish power structures. This powerful figure had previously held the office of High Priest. Annas questioned Jesus about His teachings and His disciples. Jesus simply stated that His teachings were well known. He had taught publicly in the synagogues and at the Temple. He said that, instead of questioning Him, Annas should be questioning those who heard Him. An official who was standing nearby struck Jesus in the face for His response. Jesus defended Himself, saying that He had spoken the truth and didn't deserve to be treated in this way.

#193—Jesus' Trial before Caiaphas (Matthew 26:57-68; Mark 14:53-65; Luke 22:54, 63-65; John 18:24).

Since Annas could make no progress with Jesus, he sent Jesus on to Caiaphas, the acting High Priest. Caiaphas had gathered the chief priests and the Jewish ruling council known as the Sanhedrin. Before these men Jesus would receive His official, though superficial, religious trial. The Sanhedrin wanted to kill Jesus, but they struggled to find any legal grounds for their actions. Many witnesses testified against Jesus, but their testimonies were inconsistent. Finally, two false witnesses declared that Jesus had threatened to destroy the Temple and then rebuild it in three days. Since even this testimony was without weight, Caiaphas finally questioned Jesus directly. He told Jesus to defend Himself against His accusers, but Jesus remained silent.

As a last resort, Caiaphas ordered Jesus under oath to state whether or not He was the Messiah, the Son of God. Jesus said, "I am!" He then added that at a future day the people would see Him sitting at the right hand of God in heaven. This bold declaration of His authority and deity was too much for Caiaphas. He tore his robe as a display of his distress over Jesus' statement and accused Jesus of blasphemy. No more witnesses were needed. Jesus' own words were enough to condemn Him, contrary to Jewish law. The Sanhedrin demanded that Jesus die. Some of these religious leaders spit in Jesus' face, while others slapped Him or struck Him with their fists. The guards blindfolded Jesus, beat Him, and mocked Him. The one who had come to show us God's grace was treated with unbelievable disgrace. The one who had the power to command angels submitted to the brutal beatings of wicked men. But this was just the beginning of Jesus' sufferings.

#194—PETER DENIES JESUS THREE TIMES (MATTHEW 26:69-75; MARK 14:66-72; LUKE 22:55-62; JOHN 18:15-18, 25-27).

Although the disciples had abandoned Jesus in the Garden of Gethsemane, Peter and John followed Him and His captors at a distance. John apparently had some connections with the High Priest's family, and so was admitted into Caiaphas' courtyard during Jesus' trial. John arranged to have Peter join him there. When Peter entered the courtyard, a servant girl recognized him as one of Jesus' disciples. Cowering before this little girl, Peter denied any association with Jesus. Sitting by an open fire with some of the guards, Peter was again asked if he was one of Jesus' disciples. For the second time Peter denied knowing Jesus. A little later several others gathered around Peter and accused him of being one of Jesus' followers. Peter protested, stating with an oath that he did not know Jesus. At that moment a rooster crowed. At that moment Jesus, who was within eyesight of Peter, looked at His disciple. At that moment Peter remembered how Jesus had warned that he would deny Jesus three times. Peter left the courtyard and wept bitterly over his failure to stand up for his Master.

#195—JESUS' TRIAL BEFORE THE SANHEDRIN (MATTHEW 27:1-2; MARK 15:1; LUKE 22:66-71).

As dawn began to break, the religious leaders gathered again to pronounce Jesus' final sentence. Jesus must die! Once again they asked Jesus if He was the Messiah, the Son of God. Jesus once again affirmed His identity. The religious phase of Jesus' trial came to an end. In the minds of the religious leaders, Jesus deserved the death penalty. But because Judea was under Roman jurisdiction, only the Roman governor, Pontius Pilate, could execute criminals. Therefore, the Jewish leaders took Jesus to stand trial before Pilate.

♙196—JUDAS' DEATH (MATTHEW 27:3-10).

While Jesus' religious trial unfolded, His betrayer looked on. It's impossible for us to know what thoughts raced through Judas' tortured mind. When it became apparent that Jesus was condemned to die, Judas was overcome with remorse. He tried to return the thirty pieces of silver that the religious leaders had given him for betraying Jesus. Judas knew that Jesus was innocent. No amount of money could cover Judas' horrific act. The religious leaders were unimpressed with Judas' late show of regret. Judas took the handful of silver coins and threw them into the Temple. He then went out and hanged himself. This man, who had walked with Jesus, witnessed His miracles, and listened to His teachings, now ended his life in disgrace. He will forever endure God's judgment. His life will ever serve as a warning to all who have heard the good news of Jesus and who turn away unchanged. The chief priests picked up the thirty pieces of silver which they used to purchase a plot of ground for a cemetery. It became known as the Field of Blood.

♙197—JESUS' FIRST TRIAL BEFORE PILATE (MATTHEW 27:11-14; MARK 15:2-5; LUKE 23:1-5; JOHN 18:28-38).

The Jewish leaders presented Jesus to the Roman governor, Pontius Pilate, for sentencing. Pilate asked Jesus, "Are you the king of the Jews?" Apparently, the Jewish leaders had charged Jesus with attempting to rebel against Rome, knowing that a charge of religious blasphemy wouldn't hold up in a Roman court. Jesus declared that He was indeed the king of the Jews, saying that His kingdom was not of this world. He had raised no army nor resisted arrest. His kingdom, Jesus stated, was a spiritual kingdom, a kingdom of truth. Pilate concluded that Jesus was no threat to Roman authority, and told the religious leaders that there was no basis for their case against Him.

The religious leaders protested. They claimed that Jesus had been stirring up trouble everywhere by His teachings and they accused Him of numerous crimes. Jesus stood silent before them. Pilate was amazed that Jesus didn't attempt to defend Himself before the Jewish leaders and encouraged Jesus to speak in His defense. Jesus, however, remained silent.

198—JESUS' TRIAL BEFORE HEROD (LUKE 23:6-12).

While the Jewish leaders were bringing their accusations against Jesus in Pilate's presence, they mentioned Galilee. When Pilate learned that Jesus came from Galilee, he decided to hand Jesus over to Herod Antipas. Herod was the man who had arrested and eventually executed John the Baptist. He had legal jurisdiction over Galilee, and had previously expressed a desire to see Jesus. Apparently Herod and Pilate worked under a strained relationship, as is often the case when two conflicting political authorities come side by side. In order to show his good intentions, Pilate sent Jesus to Herod, who was in Jerusalem for the Feast of Passover.

Herod was delighted to have an opportunity to see Jesus. He hoped that Jesus would perform a miracle for him. Herod questioned Jesus over and over again, but Jesus refused to speak even a word to Herod. Herod listened to the accusations of the religious leaders and finally decided to make sport of his silent victim. Herod's soldiers mocked and ridiculed Jesus. They then draped an elegant robe over Jesus' shoulders and sent Him back to Pilate.

#199—JESUS' SECOND TRIAL BEFORE PILATE (MATTHEW 27:15-26; MARK 15:6-15; LUKE 23:13-25; JOHN 18:39-40).

Once again Jesus stood before Pontius Pilate. Would Pilate have the backbone to do what was right and release Jesus, or would he cave in to the mounting political pressures that surrounded Jesus' case? Pilate made an attempt to appease the Jewish leaders while at the same time securing Jesus' freedom. It was Pilate's custom during the Passover feast to release one political prisoner chosen by the crowd. Pilate had determined that Jesus was innocent of any real crime. He informed the Jewish leaders that he intended to simply punish Jesus and let Him go. The Jewish leaders, of course, would not agree to this lenient approach. As an alternative, Pilate proposed to the gathering crowd that they choose between Jesus and a murderer named Barabbas to be released according to the custom. He knew that Jesus was popular with the crowd, and thought the crowd would call for Jesus' release. While Pilate awaited the crowd's response, his wife sent him a message. She had had a dream about Jesus and warned her husband not to have anything to do with His death. In the meantime the religious leaders influenced the crowd to call for Barabbas' release and Jesus' death. "Crucify him!" they shouted. The decision belonged to Pilate. How would he proceed? In a hollow act of defiance,

Pilate took a basin of water and washed his hands in front of the crowd, claiming innocence regarding Jesus' sentence.

⅊200—Jesus is Mocked by the Roman Soldiers (Matthew 27:27-30; Mark 15:16-19; John 19:1-3).

Pilate decided to have Jesus taken away and beaten before sentencing Him. Jesus had already been mocked and beaten by the Jewish authorities. Now, the Roman soldiers took their turn at making great sport of Jesus. They flogged Him mercilessly. They twisted together a crown made of thorns and forced it on His head. They placed a purple robe on Him, mocking His claim to royalty. They spit on Him and repeatedly struck Him in the face. We can't begin to imagine the brutality that Jesus silently endured at the hands of these ruthless soldiers. When they were finished, they ushered Jesus back to Pilate.

⅊201—Jesus is Presented to the Jews by Pilate (John 19:4-16).

Pilate now led Jesus, beaten nearly beyond recognition, before the swelling crowd. Once again Pilate stated that he found no basis for the charges leveled against Jesus. He attempted to exclude himself from any further dealings with Jesus, but the Jewish leaders insisted that Jesus must die for claiming to be the Son of God. Hearing this claim, Pilate became fearful. He took Jesus back inside and questioned Him about His origin. Jesus refused to answer. Pilate insisted that he had the authority to send

Jesus to the cross. At this, Jesus told Pilate that he had no authority apart from what was granted from God. John's Gospel tells us that Pilate attempted to set Jesus free, but the Jewish leaders accused him of being an enemy of Caesar. After all, Jesus claimed to be a king, and only Caesar was truly king in the eyes of loyal Romans. Hearing this threat, Pilate brought Jesus forward. Sitting at the official seat of judgment, Pilate presented Jesus to the Jewish leaders, saying, "Shall I crucify your king?" The Jews shouted that they were loyal to Caesar, not Jesus. Finally, Pilate sent Jesus away to be crucified.

#202—JESUS IS LED AWAY TO BE CRUCIFIED (MATTHEW 27:31-34; MARK 15:20-23; LUKE 23:26-31; JOHN 19:17).

The soldiers removed the purple robe from Jesus' back and replaced it with a cross. It was customary for convicted criminals to carry their own cross to the place of execution. Jesus, badly beaten, stumbled under the weight of His cross. The soldiers pulled a man named Simon from the crowd and forced him to carry Jesus' cross to the hill called Golgotha, or the Place of the Skull. As Jesus took each torturous step, a crowd followed along. While many in the crowd probably mocked Jesus, some of the women mourned loudly over Him. Jesus turned to these women and warned them to mourn for themselves and their children because His sentence would only bring further disaster on Jerusalem and its inhabitants. Jesus must have ached deeply for His people all along the path to Golgotha.

#203—The Crucifixion—Before the Sixth Hour (Matthew 27:35-44; Mark 15:24-32; Luke 23:32-43; John 19:18-27).

Crucifixion was a horrible punishment. Victims of this form of execution were nailed hand and foot to a cross where they slowly bled and suffocated to death, often over a period of days. In addition to the physical pain of crucifixion, the victim had to endure the ridicule of the executioners and passers-by. Jesus endured even greater suffering on the cross. There He took the sins of the world on Himself. There He experienced the unspeakable agony of separation from the Father.

When Jesus arrived at Golgotha, the soldiers nailed Him to the cross. Like a common criminal, He was crucified between two thieves. While the soldiers carried out their dark duty, Jesus prayed for their forgiveness. The soldiers then divided Jesus' clothing among them. Jesus' only earthly possession of any value was a seamless robe. The soldiers decided to keep this robe in one piece and cast lots to decide who would win this prize. Pilate had Jesus' crime etched on a board and nailed to the top of His cross. It read, "This is Jesus of Nazareth, the King of the Jews."

As people passed by, they hurled their insults at Jesus. They taunted Him, saying that if He was indeed the Messiah, He should show His miraculous power by coming down from the cross. The soldiers, and even the two thieves who were crucified with Jesus, chimed in with their verbal abuse. Eventually, one of the two thieves saw something unique in Jesus. By faith he asked

Jesus to remember him in the kingdom. Jesus assured this penitent thief that they would enter paradise together that very day.

Several women who had followed and supported Jesus during His public ministry stood by, witnessing the agony of His death. Among those women was Jesus' mother, Mary. As predicted, a sword was piercing her heart as she watched her son die. With what little breath He had, Jesus spoke to His dear mother. He committed Mary to His disciple John's care, and instructed John to treat Mary as his own mother.

#204—THE CRUCIFIXION—AFTER THE SIXTH HOUR (MATTHEW 27:45-56; MARK 15:33-41; LUKE 23:44-49; JOHN 19:28-37).

Jesus had already been on the cross for several hours. From noon until three o'clock an eerie darkness covered the land. It appeared that God had turned His back on His Son. Jesus sensed this hellish separation from the Father and cried out, "My God, my God, why have you forsaken me?" What agony Jesus must have experienced for our sake. Some of those standing near thought Jesus was calling for help. Jesus did say, "I thirst," so they lifted a sponge soaked with vinegar to relieve His parched throat. Jesus knew that He had now completed His mission. He declared from the cross, "It is finished," and then said to God the Father, "Into your hands I commit my spirit." With these final words Jesus died. In reality, no one could take His life from Him. He willingly gave His life for us.

Jesus' death was accompanied by some unusual occurrences. First, the curtain that divided the holy place from the most holy place in the Temple tore in two from top to bottom. Jesus had opened the way of access to God. Second, an earthquake rumbled through the land. Third, some tombs nearby broke open and their occupants were raised from the dead. Jesus' death was so unique that even one of the hardened soldiers who watched the crucifixion was frightened and declared, "Surely this man was the Son of God." Others who witnessed Jesus' death mourned, especially the women who had followed Jesus. To their eternal credit, they stayed near the cross until the bitter end.

Since victims of crucifixion often lasted for several days in agony on a cross, and since it was the day before the Sabbath, the Jewish leaders requested that the Romans hasten the death of the three who were crucified that day. This was done by breaking the victim's legs, making it impossible for the victim to sustain his weight and continue breathing. The soldiers followed through with this request, breaking the legs of the two thieves. But by then Jesus had already died. To confirm Jesus' death, one of the soldiers pierced His side with a spear, releasing a flow of blood mixed with water. This proved that Jesus was indeed dead.

₱205—JESUS' BURIAL (MATTHEW 27:57-61; MARK 15:42-47; LUKE 23:50-56; JOHN 19:38-42).

Jesus did have some influential friends. One such follower was Joseph, a man from Arimathea. Joseph was a wealthy member of the Jewish ruling council and had disagreed with that body's verdict on Jesus. Now Joseph went boldly to Pilate and requested possession of Jesus' body. When Pilate had confirmed that Jesus was dead he granted Joseph's request. Then Joseph along with Nicodemus, who had earlier interviewed Jesus and learned about the new birth, took Jesus' body down from the cross. They wrapped the body in linen burial cloth and applied various scented spices. Joseph owned a newly cut tomb in a garden near the place of crucifixion. He placed Jesus' body in his own tomb and rolled a large stone in front of the door of the tomb. By now it was almost sundown. The Sabbath day would soon begin. Two women observed the burial procedure intently— Mary Magdalene and another friend named Mary. After Jesus was buried, these women went home and prepared spices and perfumes to further anoint Jesus' body after the Sabbath day.

▯206—THE TOMB IS SEALED (MATTHEW 27:62-66).

The next day the religious leaders went to Pilate with an additional request. It occurred to them that Jesus had predicted He would come to life on the third day after His death. If Jesus' disciples stole His body from the tomb, there would be no end to the damage that a resurrection story might produce. So Pilate sent a contingent of soldiers who sealed the tomb, presumably checking the tomb first to ensure that the body was still there. They also posted a guard to prevent anyone from disturbing the tomb. All their precautions, however, couldn't prevent what did happen the next morning, something that none of them could have anticipated. The tomb would be empty, not because Jesus' disciples would steal the body but because Jesus would rise victoriously from the grave.

The Resurrection

The resurrection of Jesus Christ is foundational to the Christian faith. Its historical reality is central to all that Jesus taught and did. Without the resurrection, Jesus' earthly ministry has no meaning. But because Jesus is alive, He is worthy of our highest praise and our deepest devotion. The four Gospels provide vivid and sometimes seemingly conflicting details about the flurry of activities on that resurrection day. These accounts do not contradict each other—the record is cohesive. However, it's difficult to piece the information together with certainty. Nevertheless, we do know enough about the first resurrection Sunday and its subsequent events to arrive at a reasonable outline of Jesus' last days on earth.

#207—MARY MAGDALENE VISITS THE TOMB (JOHN 20:1-2).

It seems that none of Jesus' followers understood that He would rise from the dead. After Jesus' death and burial, some of the women prepared spices and perfumes for anointing Jesus' body at the earliest opportunity. Apparently they had arranged to meet at Jesus' tomb once the Sabbath day had ended. Mary Magdalene was the first to arrive. It was still very early in the morning, so early that the darkness of the night hadn't yet dissipated. When Mary arrived at Jesus' tomb she discovered that the stone had been removed from the entrance. Instead of waiting for the other women to arrive, Mary ran to find Peter and John. She assumed that someone had come in the night and removed Jesus' body.

¶208—PETER AND JOHN VISIT THE TOMB (JOHN 20:3-10).

Peter and John ran to the tomb. John arrived first and looked inside. By now the early morning light made it possible for him to see the burial linens lying in the tomb. When Peter arrived he went into the tomb and likewise saw the burial cloth as well as the cloth that had covered Jesus' head. Surprisingly, this particular piece of cloth was folded neatly and set apart from the rest of the burial linens. Whatever took place in the tomb that morning had not been done in haste. John followed Peter in entering into the tomb. Both could see that Jesus' body was gone. Peter and John returned to the home in which they were staying, perplexed but with a growing sense of faith.

¶209—MARY MAGDALENE AND THE WOMEN SEE THE ANGELS (MATTHEW 28:1-8; MARK 16:1-8; LUKE 24:1-8; JOHN 20:11-13).

Meanwhile, the other women were making their way to Jesus' tomb with their anointing spices in hand. They talked about who might roll the heavy stone away from the door of the tomb so that they could care for Jesus' body. To their surprise, when they arrived at the tomb the stone had already been removed. There had been an earthquake earlier in the morning which had terrified the guards. The guards had probably looked inside the tomb and then left the scene to report to the authorities that Jesus' body was gone. Actually, the earthquake was produced by an angel that had opened the sealed tomb.

The women, now joined by Mary Magdalene, entered the open tomb and found it empty. Suddenly, two angels appeared. The women were understandably frightened, but the angels assured them that they did not need to be afraid. Jesus had risen from the dead. The angels instructed the women to go tell the disciples, especially Peter, that Jesus was alive. He would meet them again in Galilee. The women left the tomb, still afraid but now filled with joy as well.

#210—JESUS APPEARS TO MARY MAGDALENE (MARK 16:9; JOHN 20:14-17).

While the other women went to tell the disciples about Jesus' resurrection, Mary Magdalene lingered at the tomb weeping. Turning around, she saw through her tear filled eyes a man whom she assumed was a caretaker for the garden. The man asked Mary why she was crying. Mary, not yet grasping the fact that Jesus was alive, asked the man to show her where Jesus' body had been taken. The man then simply spoke her name, "Mary." At this, Mary Magdalene recognized the man. It was Jesus! Mary, full of joy and amazement, must have fallen before Jesus and grasped his feet, never wanting to let Him go. Jesus tenderly told Mary to stop clinging to Him. He could not stay with her and His other followers indefinitely. He must go back to His Father in heaven. Mary Magdalene is credited with being the first of Jesus' followers to see Him alive again.

#211—JESUS APPEARS TO THE WOMEN (MATTHEW 28:9-10).

The other women who had gone to the tomb that morning were not far away. It may be that they heard Mary talking with someone and came back to see if everything was alright. They, too, saw Jesus and fell at His feet. Jesus encouraged them not to be afraid. Like the angels, Jesus instructed the women to tell His disciples that He was alive and would spend time with them again in Galilee.

#212—THE WOMEN REPORT TO THE DISCIPLES (MARK 16:10-11; LUKE 24:9-11; JOHN 20:18).

Mary Magdalene and the other women went quickly to the disciples and told them that the tomb was empty. Even more, they had seen and talked with Jesus. He was alive! But the disciples were not convinced. They did not yet understand that Jesus had to rise from the dead.

#213—PETER RETURNS TO THE TOMB (LUKE 24:12).

Peter, however, ran back to the tomb. If Jesus was alive, Peter wanted to see Him. When he arrived at the empty tomb, Peter again saw the linen burial cloth, but he didn't see Jesus. He left more perplexed than ever.

#214—THE GUARDS REPORT TO THE JEWISH LEADERS (MATTHEW 28:11-15).

Meanwhile the guards, who had been stunned when the angel moved the stone away from the door of the tomb, had gone to report what had happened. The chief priests and elders must have been dumbfounded. Rather than repent at the news of the resurrection, they set about devising a plan to explain away the empty tomb. They bribed the guards and told them to report that Jesus' disciples had stolen the body. These hardened religious leaders also promised to let Pilate in on this story in order to protect the guards from certain punishment. Whether they ever did so is not known. We do know that the guards obeyed the chief priests and elders. The rumor about the disciples stealing Jesus' body was the primary explanation used by those who chose to discount the resurrection in that day. This explanation is still used today by many who don't want to believe in Jesus. But Jesus was alive, regardless of what the religious leaders wanted to believe.

#215—JESUS APPEARS TO TWO MEN ON THE EMMAUS ROAD (MARK 16:12-13; LUKE 24:13-35).

On the day of Jesus' resurrection, two of His followers were walking from Jerusalem to the outlying town of Emmaus. Along the way they talked about the unusual events of the past few days, including the reports of Jesus' resurrection. Then Jesus came along side of them, but they didn't recognize Him. Jesus may have hidden His identity from them for the time being. Certainly these men weren't expecting to encounter Jesus. Jesus asked the men what they were discussing, and they described to this stranger the life and death of Jesus. They also told their traveling companion how they had received reports from some of the women that Jesus was alive. As they walked along, Jesus, "beginning with Moses and all the prophets," unfolded the Scriptural teachings about the Messiah. The Messiah had to die and rise again. What a Bible lesson that must have been!

When the two travelers arrived at Emmaus they invited the stranger to stay with them since evening was quickly approaching. Jesus accepted their invitation. At dinner, Jesus blessed and broke the bread. At that moment the two men recognized Jesus, but Jesus disappeared from their sight. The two men began to chide each other for not recognizing Jesus sooner. After all, their hearts had sensed something unique about this stranger while Jesus had been talking with them along the way. Although it was late in the evening, the two men hurried back to Jerusalem and found Jesus' disciples. They discovered that Jesus had appeared to Peter earlier in the day. The two travelers then described what had taken place along the road to Emmaus. They now knew that Jesus was alive.

216—JESUS APPEARS TO THE TEN DISCIPLES (MARK 16:14; LUKE 24:36-44; JOHN 20:19-24).

Jesus' disciples and other followers were huddled behind locked doors the night of the resurrection, fearful of what the religious authorities might do to them. They were busily talking about the events of that remarkable day. Suddenly Jesus appeared among them. He said, "Peace be with you." Now the disciples were even more frightened. Was this a ghost? Jesus reassured them that He was really alive. He showed them His hands and feet. He let them touch Him. He ate with them. He explained the Scriptures to them, including the necessity of His death and resurrection. The disciples were too full of amazement and joy to believe quite yet. Jesus gently rebuked their lack of faith, and then again granted His peace. He told these faithful followers that He was sending them out on a mission to declare God's forgiveness. Then Jesus prepared them to receive the Holy Spirit by breathing on them. In addition to some close friends, all of Jesus' disciples were present that evening except Thomas.

#217—JESUS APPEARS TO THE ELEVEN DISCIPLES (JOHN 20:25-31).

The disciples who were present when Jesus appeared to them on the night of the resurrection went and told Thomas the good news. They had seen Jesus. Jesus was alive! Thomas, however, refused to believe. He demanded physical evidence. He declared that, unless he could see the nail marks in Jesus' hands, touch those marks with his finger, and put his hand in Jesus' side, he would not believe. A full week went by. The disciples had again gathered together and this time Thomas was present. Once again Jesus appeared to them and said, "Peace be with you." Then Jesus turned to Thomas. He invited Thomas to touch His hands and side. He wanted Thomas to stop doubting and to believe. Thomas acknowledged his faith in Jesus, exclaiming, "My Lord and my God!" Jesus then affirmed Thomas' faith. In addition, Jesus spoke a word of blessing on others who would believe in Him without the benefit of seeing Him. That blessing extends to Jesus' followers today. We who have never seen Jesus with our eyes but have believed in Him with our hearts have received a special blessing from Jesus Christ!

John's Gospel states that, during His earthly ministry, Jesus performed numerous miracles in the presence of His disciples, many of which went unrecorded. The four Gospels provide only a limited description of Jesus' works. However, what is recorded is sufficient for our faith. We must believe in Jesus and, by believing, we receive eternal life in His name.

#218—JESUS APPEARS TO THE DISCIPLES AT THE SEA OF GALILEE (JOHN 21:1-25).

John's Gospel alone records a very tender scene in the post-resurrection life of Jesus Christ. Jesus said that He would meet with His disciples in Galilee. The disciples made their way north from Jerusalem to this familiar territory along the shore of the Sea of Galilee. While they waited for Jesus to appear, Peter, Thomas, Nathanael, James, John, and two other disciples decided to go fishing. They set out in a boat and fished all night without catching anything. At daybreak these luckless fishermen saw a man on shore who asked if they had caught any fish. Since these disciples had been unsuccessful all night, the man on shore instructed them to cast their net on the other side of the boat. Just as had happened when Jesus originally called

Peter to follow Him, the net came up full of fish. At this point John recognized the man on shore and told Peter that it was Jesus. Peter was so eager to see Jesus again that he jumped into the water and swam to shore.

The rest of the disciples towed the boat and their catch to shore, where they found that Jesus already had fish cooking over an open fire. He invited them to enjoy breakfast with Him, giving them bread and fish. This must have been the most satisfying breakfast they had ever enjoyed because they were in the presence of the resurrected Christ.

After breakfast, Jesus took Peter aside. It was true that Peter had denied Jesus three times. Now Jesus invited Peter to reaffirm his love three times. Furthermore, three times Jesus commanded Peter to feed His sheep. Jesus went on to warn Peter that commitment to following Him meant Peter would one day be led off to die as a martyr. Jesus then invited Peter to follow Him. In this way Jesus lovingly reinstated Peter to a place of useful service.

Peter must have welcomed Jesus' forgiveness and His confidence in him. But looking behind him, Peter saw John following along. He asked Jesus what would become of John. Jesus said that even if John lived until Jesus' return, Peter must focus on his own calling. Once again Jesus said to Peter, "You follow me." John explains in his Gospel that some people had mistaken Jesus' statement as a prediction that John would not die before Jesus returned, but Jesus merely contrasted the two paths set before these two disciples. We must learn to follow Jesus along the path marked for us. Others will experience their own triumphs and tragedies, but we must all remain faithful to Christ's calling in our lives. John concluded his Gospel by reminding us that Jesus did many other marvelous things during His time on earth. The world couldn't possibly contain all the books necessary to adequately record the life and work of Jesus Christ.

#219—JESUS GIVES HIS GREAT COMMISSION (MATTHEW 28:16-20; MARK 16:15-18; LUKE 24:45-48).

Jesus appeared to His followers over a period of forty days following His resurrection. On one occasion He met them at a designated mountain in Galilee where He gave them His Great Commission. There the disciples worshiped Jesus, although some were still struggling to understand. Jesus told His disciples that all authority in heaven and earth had been granted to Him. He, therefore, commissioned His disciples to go to all nations and make more disciples. They were to proclaim the good news, teach God's truth, call people to repentance, and baptize converts. This task would require supernatural power, so Jesus assured His disciples that He would always be with them. We must depend on the power of God to help us accomplish the work of God. Jesus' Great Commission is still our mission today. We have good news to share. Jesus is God. He died for our sins. He rose from the dead. Salvation is available through faith in Him and Him alone. This is the gospel of Jesus Christ.

₱220—JESUS ASCENDS INTO HEAVEN (MARK 16:19-20; LUKE 24:49-53).

Jesus met with His disciples on one final occasion. Outside Jerusalem, on the Mount of Olives, Jesus instructed His disciples to wait in the city for the outpouring of the Holy Spirit. It would be the Holy Spirit who would empower Jesus' followers to accomplish their task. Jesus then pronounced a blessing on His followers. At that moment Jesus ascended into heaven where He was seated at the right hand of God the Father. The disciples paused in worship of Jesus as their God. Then they went back into Jerusalem full of joy. Soon Jesus' followers would experience the outpouring of God's Holy Spirit and enter into the task Jesus had set before them. They would powerfully share the love of Jesus Christ. These men and women were each transformed by Jesus Christ. They were no longer cowards, but courageous witnesses. They had been with Jesus and their lives would never be the same. When we receive Jesus by faith, we too have a mission to fulfill. When we encounter Jesus, we too can never be the same.